Giles

COMPUTATION & COGNITION

Proceedings of the First
NEC Research Symposium

COMPUTATION & COGNITION

Proceedings of the First NEC Research Symposium

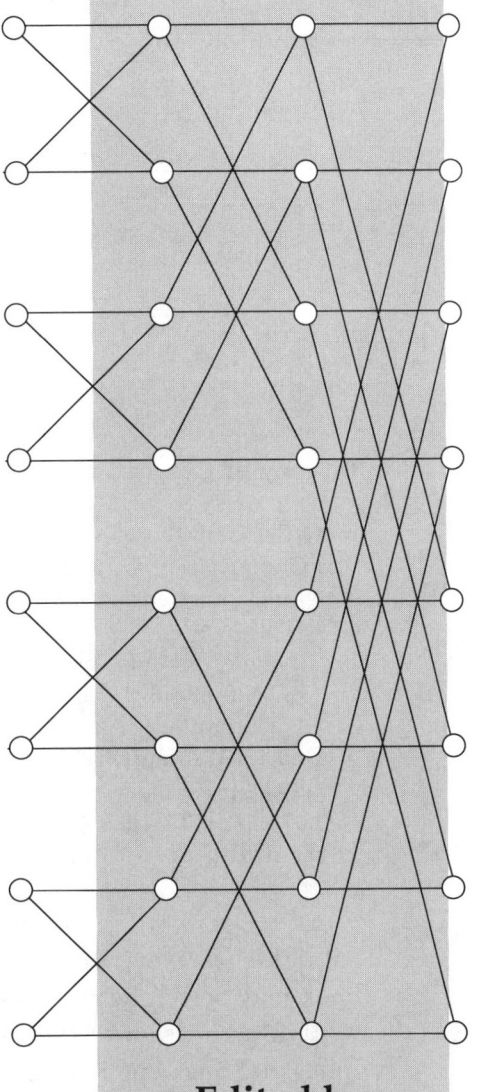

Society for Industrial and Applied Mathematics
Philadelphia

Edited by
C. W. Gear

Library of Congress Cataloging-in-Publication Data

NEC Research Symposium (1st : 1989 : Princeton, N.J.)
    Computation & cognition : proceedings of the First NEC Research Symposium / edited by C.W. Gear.
    p.   cm.
    Includes bibliographical references.
    ISBN 0-89871-272-6
    1. Computer science–Research–Congresses. I. Gear, C. William (Charles William), 1935– . II. Title. III. Title: Computation and cognition.
QA76.27.N43   1989
004'.072–dc20   91-18523

All rights reserved. Printed in the United States of America. No part of this book may be reproduced, stored, or transmitted in any manner without the written permission of the Publisher. For information, write the Society for Industrial and Applied Mathematics, 3600 University City Science Center, Philadelphia, PA 19104-2688.

©1991 by the Society for Industrial and Applied Mathematics.

Preface

NEC, through its Central Research Laboratories in Japan and the NEC Research Institute in Princeton, NJ, is organizing annual research symposia on topics in computer science and related area.

Early progress in computing, computer design, and computer science was characterized by fruitful interactions between people from many disciplines. A goal of the new NEC Research Institute is to foster interactions between people from a variety of disciplines to spawn ideas and techniques that will provide the basis for computing and computers decades hence. This symposium series will bring together leading researchers from these disciplines for a few days of intense interactions.

The first NEC Research Symposium was held in Princeton on May 1-2, *1990* in conjunction with the dedication of the new Research Institute facility. The conference, through its theme Computation and Cognition, explored the relations between different modes of computation, and brought together views of the computation process from different disciplines. Physics, where spin glass models display surprising properties and cellular automata have been used for hydrodynamic calculations, biology, with its new understandings of the computational process in neural systems ("wetware"), artificial neural networks, and electrical engineering, as well as the traditional computer science areas of architecture, artificial intelligence, and learning theory, are represented in these proceedings.

The papers in this volume reveal the excitement present in many disciplines over the computational possibilities of new models; the belief that a better understanding of more "intelligent" computation will only come about through a symbiosis of the different models of computation now being explored, models that are a far greater leap from the von Neuman model than the parallel models that have been the focus of much recent activity in computer science. Will these new models yield insights that will lead to the next revolution in computing? We do not know; the purpose of this and subsequent volumes is to examine these issues and challenge the community to consider new possibilities.

As with any symposium, many people contributed greatly to its success, and it is not possible to acknowledge all, but I would like to mention particularly Dawon Kahng, President of the NEC Research Institute, who lead the effort to organize the symposium, Peter Wolff, Fellow of the Institute, who chaired the program committee, and Steve Oppen, Vice President for Administration, who handled the local arrangements.

C. W. Gear
Princeton, 1990

Foreword

The NEC Corporation is proud to publish the NEC Research Symposium proceedings. The first symposium marks the dedication of the facility for the NEC Research Institute. The Institute, founded in 1988, conducts long-term, basic research in sciences underlying the computer and communication technologies of the future. The goal of the Institute is to generate significant new knowledge and concepts, and to flourish as a world-class scientific research laboratory. All research results are to be published in the open literature. The Institute seeks close collaborations with universities and other research institutions, and anticipates making an important contribution to the basic research community, and through future applications of its results, to the quality of human life.

A focus of the Institute's work is integrated research in the physical and computer sciences. Close cooperation between scientists in the two areas is strongly encouraged in the expectation that major future advances in computing will emerge from better understanding by computer scientists of physical phenomena that are the basis of computing, and by physical scientists of the nature and needs of advanced computing.

A distinctive feature of the Institute's work environment is the collegial and participative organizational structure, intended to promote individual creativity. Responsibility for scientific direction rests largely with a Board of Fellows, a group of the Institute's most distinguished Members. Adequate funding and resources offer Members the freedom to pursue independent research.

The first symposium has reflected the general, basic research character of the NEC Research Institute. The second symposium is scheduled to take place in Tokyo in 1991. The theme has been selected as "Algorithm and Architecture." From there on, the site of the annual symposium will alternate between Princeton and Tokyo.

The NEC Corporation hopes, through this series of the NEC Research Symposium and its Proceedings, to make a small but tangible contribution to the progress in computer science and eventually to the future of C&C, that is, integration of computer and communications Technologies, for the forthcoming Information Age.

                        Koji Maeda
                        Senior Executive Vice President
                        NEC Corporation
                        Tokyo, Japan
                        October, 1990

Contents

New Opportunities in Multicomputers 1
   H. T. Kung

Optical Interconnections in Computing 22
   Joseph W. Goodman

A View of Computational Learning Theory 32
   Leslie G. Valiant

Mappings Between High-Dimensional Representations
of Acoustic and Visual Speech Signals 52
   Terrence J. Sejnowski and Ben P. Yuhas

Colligation of Coupled Cortical Oscillators by the
Collapse of the Distributions of Amplitude-Dependent
Characteristic Frequencies 69
   Walter J. Freeman

Directions in Natural Language Processing 104
   Mitchell Marcus

What Does Theoretical Physics Have to Say About
Information Science? 127
   P. W. Anderson

Panel Session 137
   Chairman: Professor Amari

Chapter 1
New Opportunities in Multicomputers*

H. T. Kung[†]

Abstract

A multicomputer is a distributed memory parallel computing system made of multiple homogeneous or heterogeneous processors. Parallel machines of this kind are highly flexible in their configurations and usages, and are expected to be the mainstream high-performance computing environment of the 1990s.

Carnegie Mellon, with its competitively selected industrial partners, has two research projects in this area. The *iWarp* project has developed a single-chip building block processor for homogeneous multicomputers. Consisting of about 650,000 transistors, the iWarp processor is one of the first high-performance microprocessors specially designed for parallel processing.

The *Nectar* project has developed a high-speed network backplane for heterogeneous multicomputers. The Nectar network is made of fiber-optic links, large crossbar switches, and dedicated network coprocessors. A 26-host Nectar prototype using 100 megabits/second links is supporting research in distributed computing. The next generation Nectar, using 1 gigabits/second or higher speed fiber links, is under development.

These two efforts exemplify new opportunities in multicomputers. Homogeneous multicomputers can now take advantage of highly integrated processors such as iWarp that have been specially designed to support fast and flexible interprocessor communication needed in parallel processing. Heterogeneous multicomputers, capable of simultaneously providing different types of computing resources to meet application needs, can now be based on a general high-speed network backplane such as Nectar.

---

*Research supported in part by the Defense Advanced Research Projects Agency (DOD) monitored by DARPA/CMO under Contract MDA972-90-C-0035, in part by the National Science Foundation and the Defense Advanced Research Projects Agency under Cooperative Agreement NCR-8919038 with the Corporation for National Research Initiatives, and in part by the Office of Naval Research under Contract N00014-90-J-1939.

[†]School of Computer Science, Carnegie Mellon University, Pittsburgh, Pennsylvania 15213.

1 Introduction

More than 1000 supercomputers are installed worldwide as of 1990, but applications continue to demand more computing power. Computational problems in areas such as high-speed aircraft design and medical imaging, and research in advanced structural, electronic, and optical materials often require computers that are at least three orders of magnitude faster than the fastest computers presently available.

While computing demands increase rapidly, the performance of conventional, sequential computers is approaching the point of diminishing return. High-performance sequential computers today are bounded by, among other things, memory speed. However, the speed of mainstream memory technology improves slowly: one can expect at most one order of magnitude speedup in the next ten years. Parallel computers, in which a number of processors can work in parallel on their local memories for a single application, offer the only solution capable of providing orders of magnitude of improvement in computing performance without excessive cost.

There has been substantial investment in parallel processing over the past twenty years. In the past six or seven years we have seen an accelerated effort in this area. During this period, many companies started marketing parallel computer systems. Shared memory parallel computers include MIMD machines such as the Alliant, Encore, Sequent, and CRAY Y-MP. Distributed memory computers include MIMD machines such as the Transputer [16] and various hypercube systems [4], as well as SIMD machines such as the Connection Machine [28], DAP, and MasPar. Many more parallel machines of enhanced capabilities are under development. Successful use of these parallel computers has been demonstrated in a number of application areas, including scientific computing, signal and image processing, and logic simulation. For some of these applications, the available parallelism increases as the problem size expands, so it is possible to achieve close to linear speedup on parallel machines.

The next generation of parallel computers will allow easier, more efficient and more flexible use of parallelism than the present generation. To be scalable to a large number of processing nodes, new parallel computers will mainly be distributed memory machines. For programmability these machines may support various shared memory programming models. To achieve high performance, these machines will explore multiple levels and forms of parallelism, and allow heterogeneous processing nodes whenever appropriate.

These requirements for next generation parallel computers call for *multicomputers* that have high-bandwidth and low-latency internode communication capabilities. A multicomputer is said to be *homogeneous* if its processors are all of the same type; otherwise the multicomputer is said to be *heteroge-*

neous. Existing message-passing machines [16,4,27] represent a strong starting point in homogeneous multicomputers. This paper describes two new multicomputer systems, *iWarp* and *Nectar*, whose development Carnegie Mellon is currently involved with.

iWarp [7,6] is one of the first high-performance microprocessors specially designed for homogeneous multicomputers. Developed jointly with Intel, the single-chip iWarp processor has about 650,000 transistors and can sustain a very high I/O bandwidth: 320 megabytes/second I/O for inter-processor communication plus 160 megabytes/second I/O for local memory communication. In addition to the usual communication functions such as routing, iWarp is unique in that it has on-chip hardware support for systolic communication and logical channels [7]. Two 1.28 GFLOPS, 64-processor iWarp systems are operational at Carnegie Mellon. An overview of the iWarp system and its architectural innovations in interprocessor communication is given in Section 2.1.

Nectar [3] is a high-speed network backplane to connect together heterogeneous computer architectures and peripherals, to fit different needs of an application. The Nectar network is made of fiber-optic links, large crossbar switches, and dedicated network coprocessors. A 26-host Nectar prototype using 100 megabits/second links is operational at Carnegie Mellon. One of these links is a 26 km Nectar connection to a Westinghouse facility, which hosts the CRAY Y-MP of the Pittsburgh Supercomputing Center. With Network Systems Corporation, Carnegie Mellon is designing the next generation Nectar using 1 gigabits/second or higher speed fiber links. This new system will support the 800 megabits/second HIPPI (High-Performance Parallel Interface) ANSI standard, and will have a SONET interface supported by phone carriers. The gigabit Nectar system is one of the five testbeds in a US national effort to develop gigabits/second wide-area networks. The Nectar system is described in Section 3.

2 iWarp: A Building Block for Homogeneous Multicomputers

2.1 iWarp Overview

iWarp [7,6] is a distributed parallel computing system in joint development between Carnegie Mellon University and Intel Corporation since 1986. The architecture is derived from the original Warp architecture [2] developed by Carnegie Mellon. The building block of an iWarp system is the *iWarp cell*, made out of a single-chip *iWarp processor* (or *iWarp component*) connected to a local memory. Homogeneous multicomputers of different scales and topologies can be built cost-effectively by simply linking together iWarp cells. Figure 1 illustrates one possible configuration.

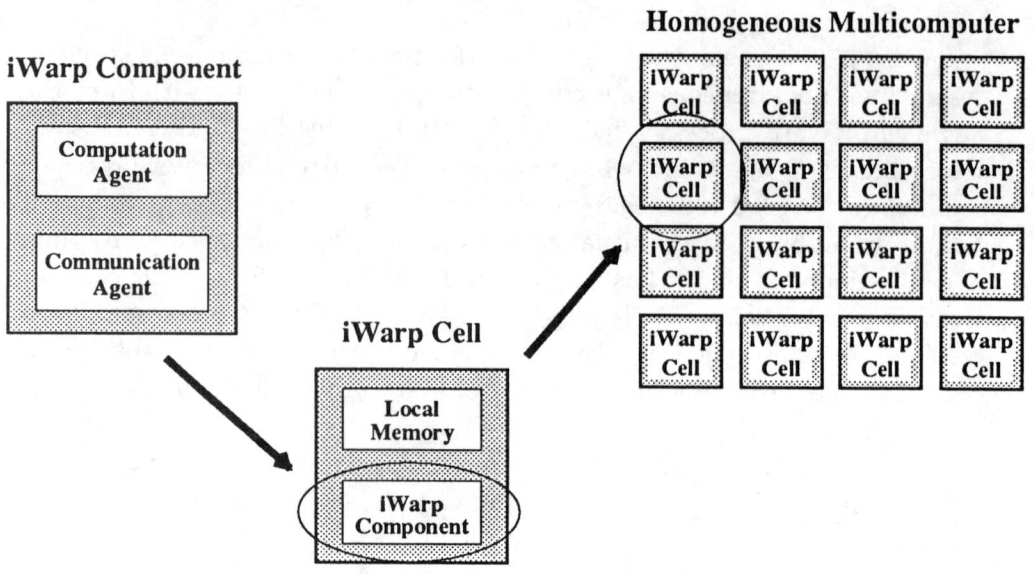

Figure 1:
iWarp cell: a building block for homogeneous multicomputers.

As shown in the figure, the iWarp processor integrates both computation and communication functions on a single VLSI component. The processor is a powerful computation engine that employs instruction-level parallelism to allow simultaneous operation of multiple functional units [9]. What makes iWarp unique, however, is its interprocessor communication capability. An iWarp processor can simultaneously communicate with a number of other iWarp processors at high speed. In addition, the iWarp processor has a highly flexible communication mechanism that can support a variety of programming models. These models include the tightly coupled parallel computing found in systolic arrays and the loosely coupled message-passing style of computation found in many other distributed memory machines. These communication capabilities allow the effective use of iWarp for a wide range of applications.

The iWarp component has two autonomous subsystems, as depicted in Figure 2. The *computation agent*, which executes programs, can deliver 20 (or 10) MFLOPS for single (or double) precision calculations plus 20 MIPS for integer/logic operations. The *communication agent*, which implements the iWarp's communication system, can sustain an aggregate intercell communication bandwidth of 320 MBytes/sec by using four input and four output busses. Furthermore, the iWarp component has a high-bandwidth

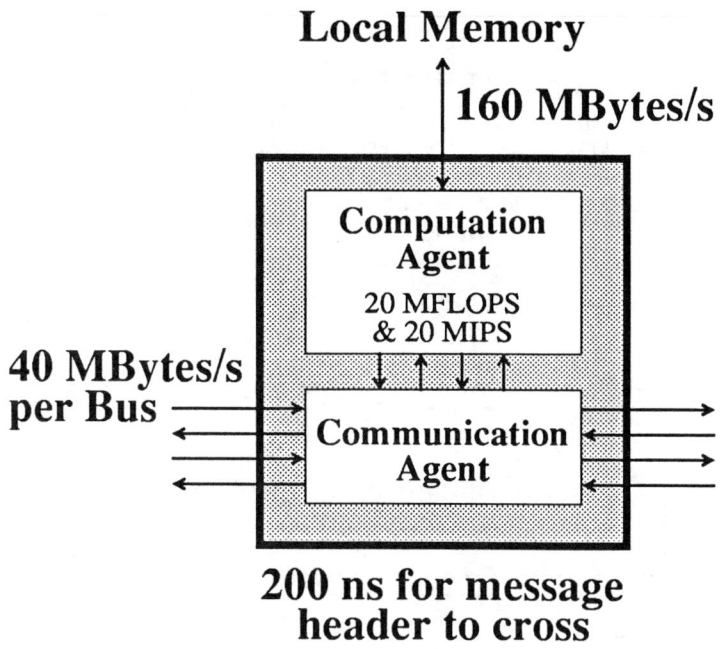

Figure 2:
iWarp component overview.

interface to the local memory, capable of transferring streams of data into or out of the communication agent at a rate of 160 MBytes/sec.

The iWarp component consists of approximately 650,000 transistors and measures about 1.4cm (551mil) on a side. Figure 3 shows a floor plan that highlights the major functional units. The iWarp component operates at a frequency of 20 MHz, with the exception that the data is transferred between processors at twice that frequency.

The software for the initial iWarp systems includes optimizing compilers for C and FORTRAN for the programming of single cells. In addition, parallel program generators are available, such as Apply [15] for image processing and AL @citeTsengAParallelizing for scientific computing, for the programming of multiple cells. These parallel program generators can automatically produce for each cell a C program augmented with explicit intercell communication instructions. A resident run-time system on each cell allows multiple light-weight threads to share physical resources, and supports systolic and memory communication (see Section 2.2.2). Included in this run-time system are the message-passing services of the Nectar communication system (see Section 3.2.2).

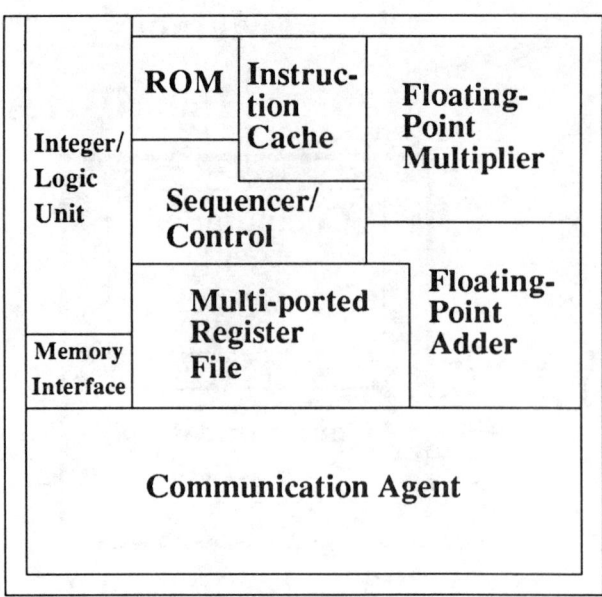

Figure 3:
Floor plan of iWarp component.

2.2 Three iWarp Architectural Innovations in Communication

iWarp has three important architectural innovations: high-bandwidth I/O, systolic communication, and logical channels [7]. These innovations are described in the next subsection.

In addition, iWarp has many of the more "traditional" communication features [6] found in previous distributed memory machines [4,26], such as support for non-neighborhood communication, message routing hardware, word-level flow control between neighboring cells, and spooling (a DMA-like mechanism for high-bandwidth communication with local memory). Together, the traditional features and the three innovations make iWarp an effective processor to implement a variety of interprocessor communication styles [19]. As a result, the iWarp component and subsystems using it are powerful building blocks for constructing many general-purpose and special-purpose computing systems [5]. These systems can achieve high-performance, while maintaining a high degree of flexibility to address different application needs.

2.2.1 High-bandwidth I/O

As shown in Figure 2, the single-chip iWarp processor can sustain a very high I/O bandwidth: 320 megabytes/second I/O for inter-processor communication plus 160 megabytes/second I/O for local memory communication.

A high-bandwidth I/O capability is extremely important for a high-performance processor. Suppose that the computation rate of the processor is increased by a factor ρ relative to the I/O bandwidth. To ensure that computation at the processor will not wait for I/O, the size of the local memory must be increased so that more data items can be "cached" locally to reduce the need for I/O. However, it has been shown [23] that the size of the local memory must increase rapidly for many important computations. For example, for matrix computation such as matrix multiplication, the local memory must be increased by a factor of $O(\rho^2)$. The corresponding factor for a d-dimensional grid computation is $O(\rho^d)$. For other more I/O intensive computations such as sorting and FFT, the memory size must be increased even more rapidly.

There are at least two problems in requiring a large local memory. First, large memory is expensive. Second, requiring the computation to be sufficiently large, in order to use a large memory, can substantially reduce the applicability of the processor.

Consequently, a high-performance processor should have a high I/O bandwidth to keep the value of ρ small. This is a fundamental reason why iWarp has been designed to have such a high I/O bandwidth.

2.2.2 Systolic Communication

On a multicomputer, the sending or receiving processor of a message can perform either memory or systolic communication [18], as depicted in Figure 4.

In memory communication, the entire message is buffered in the local memory of the processor before it is transmitted or after it is received. Therefore communication begins or terminates at the local memory. For conventional message-passing methods, both sending and receiving processors use memory communication. In contrast, in systolic communication, individual data items are transferred as they are produced, or are used as they are received, by the program running at the processor.

Systolic communication was motivated by systolic algorithms [21,22]. In a systolic algorithm, an array of cells perform computations on long data streams flowing through the array. To achieve high efficiency, each cell processes the data immediately as each item arrives. We can view all data sent along each directed connection in a systolic array as belonging to one message. However, instead of waiting until all the data in the message have arrived, each cell operates on the data items within a message as they arrive individually. It then sends the results of the computation to other cells on-the-fly as data of out-going messages. Therefore, each cell performs systolic communication as defined in the preceding paragraph.

Memory Communication (e.g., Message-Passing):

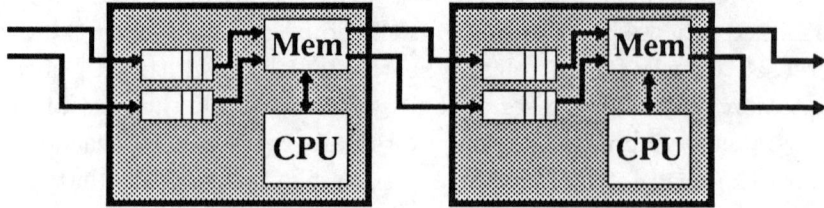

Systolic Communication:

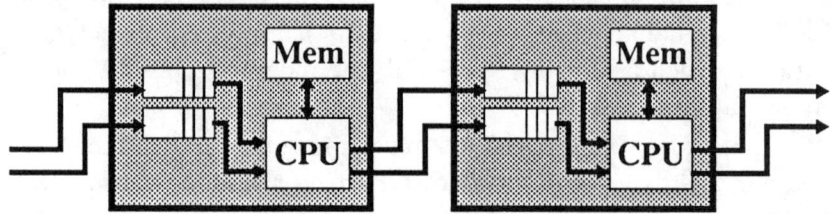

Figure 4:
Systolic vs. memory communication.

Systolic communication has the following advantages over memory communication:

- *Fine-grain communication.* The program at the sending cell can send out data items individually as soon as they are produced; similarly the program at the receiving cell can use data items individually as soon as they are received. This allows programs to communicate and synchronize with each other at word-level rather than message-level granularity. The message routing and header information overheads are not paid with each unit of synchronization. This low communication cost makes it possible for the cells to cooperate in fine-grain parallel processing.

- *Reduced access to local memory.* Incoming and outgoing data need not be buffered in a cell's local memory unless it is required by the computation. Since memory access is typically a bottleneck in a cell's performance, the reduced access to local memory may translate into increased computation performance.

- *Increased instruction-level parallelism.* At each cell, systolic inputs and outputs provide additional parallel sources of operands for instructions. These operands can help keep the multiple functional units busy and increase instruction-level parallelism. Optimizing compilers for wide-word instruction set architectures, such as the compilers for Warp and iWarp [9,24], have been developed to take advantage of this instruction-level parallelism.

- *Reduced size for local memory.* Avoiding buffering data in the local memory also reduces the memory size requirement for some applications.

iWarp supports systolic communication by exposing its low level communication mechanisms to programs. First, the communication agent supports word-level flow control between connecting cells and transfers messages word by word to implement wormhole routing [14,13]. Exposing this mechanism to the computation agents allows programs to communicate systolically. Second, a communication agent can automatically route messages to the appropriate destination without the intervention of the computation agent. By allowing the computation agent to modify the routing of messages in midstream, the program can implement some common message operations such as message concatenation or distribution efficiently. For examples the program can implement the "GetRow" and "PutRow" I/O methods [1], which have been extensively used on Warp for image processing applications.

2.2.3 Logical Channels

iWarp's third innovation in communication is logical channels. They have two important functions. First, in mapping computations onto iWarp arrays, logical channels provide a higher degree of connectivity than that achievable by physical means. Second, they provide a mechanism for delivering guaranteed communication bandwidth for classes of messages.

Increasing connectivity

When mapping computations onto iWarp arrays, it is desirable for the cells to be highly interconnected. However, the number of physical connections available on a cell is limited by hard constraints such as the number of available pins and pads on the iWarp component. Logical channels overcome this problem by providing multiple "logical" connections over the same physical connection. In iWarp, multiple logical channels can time-multiplex a physical bus at word-level granularity. A total of twenty logical channels can be be multiplexed over the eight input and output busses in each cell.

A high degree of connectivity is useful for systolic communication. In systolic communication, a cell may need to have simultaneous connections to several cells. Without logical channels, algorithms that require more physical connections than those provided in hardware cannot be implemented. Consider, for example, mapping a hexagonal systolic array onto a 2-dimensional grid of iWarp processors. Whereas the X and Y connections of the hexagonal array map directly onto those of the iWarp array, each of the diagonal connections of the hexagonal array can be implemented on the iWarp array with one horizontal and one vertical logical channels.

In general, a high degree of connectivity is required when mapping computations onto a physical array which has quite a different intercell communication topology. Even when the computation and the physical array have exactly the same communication topology, extra connections may still be needed to route around congested or faulty cells. Extensive simulation has shown that a moderate number of logical channels (on the order of 10) can be highly effective in avoiding faulty cells [25].

Delivering guaranteed communication bandwidth

Logical channels can be used to guarantee communication bandwidth for special classes of messages between a set of selected cells. The time-multiplexing of logical channels onto physical busses uses a schedule that guarantees that no active logical channel suffers from starvation. This guarantees some minimum bandwidth to each logical channel, and thus to the messages carried by the channel. Moreover, the multiplexing of logical channels to physical busses is designed such that idle logical channels do not consume any physical bandwidth. That is, when a logical channel is inactive, the physical bandwidth reserved for it is not wasted and can be used by other logical channels.

The ability to deliver guaranteed communication bandwidth is important for both systolic and memory communication. The need in the case of systolic communication is obvious. The connection for systolic communication requires some guaranteed minimum performance to ensure effective low cost fine-grain communication. A systolic connection may exist for an indefinitely long period of time, possibly for the duration of an entire application program. If connections exclude other communication on the same bus, then cells engaged in systolic communication can potentially lock out all other messages by monopolizing the connections. It is important that some bandwidth be made available for memory communication to support system-related functions such as monitoring.

Guaranteeing communication bandwidth in the case of memory communication is less clear but nonetheless important. Messages received and sent using memory communication will complete in a bounded amount of time for a given available communication bandwidth. Provided that at least one connection from any cell to any cell can be made at any one time, all messages will eventually arrive at their destinations. However, there is little guarantee as to when a particular message will be delivered. Reserving a set of logical channels for a class of messages of bounded lengths guarantees that some minimum bandwidth is reserved for them. For example, it is useful to guarantee that special system messages can be delivered in a timely fashion. This is especially useful for debugging and diagnostic purposes.

Reserving communication resources in iWarp is modeled by the notion of *pathways*, each being a chain of linearly connected logical channels. Logical channels in a given set of pathways can be reserved to transport a class of messages between the cells connected by the pathways. Conversely, all these messages are confined to use only those logical channels within the pathways, guaranteeing the availability of the rest of the resources for other usages.

3 Nectar: A Network Backplane for Heterogeneous Multicomputers

Future high-performance computing needs will require more than just vector supercomputers or parallel architectures such as iWarp. A complementary and sometimes much smarter approach is to use *heterogeneous multicomputers* capable of simultaneously providing a variety of computer architectures to a single application. We envision such a heterogeneous environment including both conventional supercomputers and parallel computers. The parallel computers may handle parts of the application which are parallelizable while the supercomputers can deal with those parts which are vectorizable.

Key scientific advances required for realizing high-performance heterogeneous multicomputers are in high-bandwidth and low-latency networks for intersystem communication. For this, very high-speed computer networks are being developed. Taking advantage of the recent phenomenal progress in fiber-optics technology, these new networks will be orders of magnitude faster than current ones and will allow heterogeneous multicomputers to be constructed using local area or even wide area networks.

The Nectar project [3] at Carnegie Mellon is one of the first attempts in building these very high-speed networks. Nectar uses fiber-optic links, large crossbar switches, and dedicated network coprocessors. A prototype system employing 100 megabits per second (Mb/s) links has been operational since early 1989. As of spring 1990 the system has 26 hosts, and is readily extendible to 32 hosts. In addition, a 26 km Nectar connection to a Westinghouse facility, which hosts the CRAY Y-MP of the Pittsburgh Supercomputing Center, is operational. With Network Systems Corporation, Carnegie Mellon is currently designing the next-generation Nectar using 1 gigabit per second (Gb/s) or higher speed fiber links.

3.1 Heterogeneous Multicomputers

This section describes heterogeneous multicomputers and motivates the need for them from applications viewpoints. A heterogeneous multicomputer is a network-based computing environment allowing different types of computing resources cooperating on a single application. Figure 5 depicts the concept of a heterogeneous multicomputer whose nodes are various kinds of processors or devices. Note that in addition to conventional high-performance

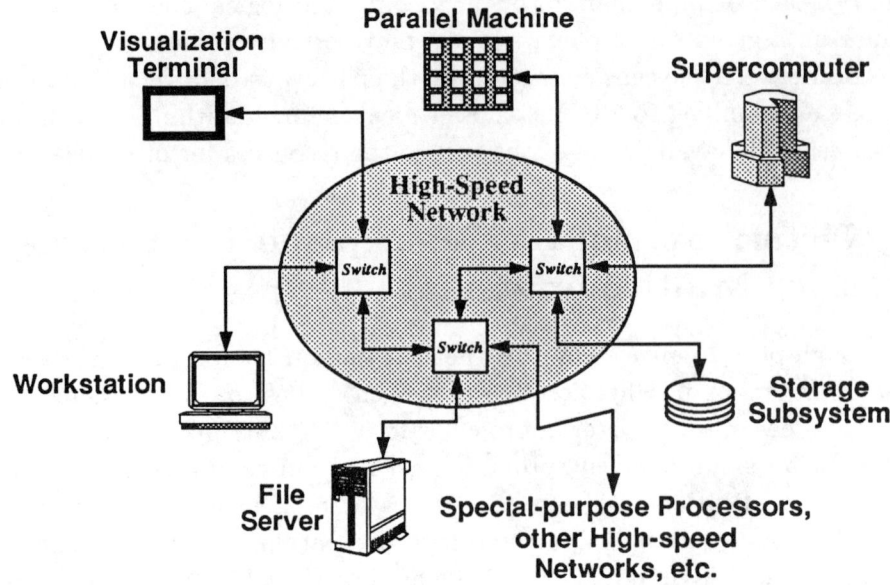

Figure 5:
Heterogeneous multicomputer.

processors, the system can include I/O nodes, special-purpose processors, and terminals for user interface.

Prior approaches in high-performance computing architectures have developed fast scalar or vector processors and homogeneous parallel machines. Each of these machine types is most suited for certain kinds of computations. For a computation which is highly parallelizable but requires only simple control, a massively parallel machine that can scale up easily with problem size is ideal. However, a parallel machine is fundamentally not suited for computations which are highly sequential; in this case fast scalar processors should be used. Similarly, while ideal for vector computations, vector machines are not cost-effective for highly sequential or parallel computations.

Heterogeneous multicomputers represent a new direction in high-performance architectures. By incorporating a variety of existing processors or devices as nodes, a heterogeneous multicomputer allows simultaneous use of the best suited architectures to carry out computations of different characteristics.

Consider, for example, a numerical simulation of a flying airplane in evaluating its design. The simulation involves two interacting, large-grain computation tasks that need to be performed simultaneously. One task is the simulation of the aircraft body structure using implicit numerical methods on irregular, coarse meshes. The other task is the simulation of air fluid around the airplane using explicit numerical methods on regular, fine meshes. It turns out that the first task is suited to a vector machine while the second task is ideal for a parallel machine. Therefore the entire simulation requires a heterogeneous multicomputer equipped with both kinds of machines as nodes. The heterogeneity is inherent in the physical world to be simulated!

Heterogeneous multicomputers are useful for applications that require information processing at multiple, qualitatively different levels [3]. For example, a computer vision system may require image processing on its raw sensor input at the lowest level, and scene recognition using a knowledge base at the highest level. A speech understanding system has a similar structure, with low-level signal processing and high-level natural language parsing. The processing required by an autonomous robot might range from handling sensor inputs to high-level planning. At the lowest levels, these applications deal with simple data structures and highly regular number-crunching algorithms. The large amount of data at high rates often requires specialized hardware. At the highest levels, these applications may use complicated symbolic data structures and data-dependent flow of control. Specialized inference engines or database machines might be appropriate for these tasks. The very nature of these applications dictates a heterogeneous hardware environment, with varied instruction sets, data representations, and performance characteristics.

3.2 Nectar System at Carnegie Mellon

To demonstrate the feasibility of constructing high-performance heterogeneous multicomputers in a general way, we have been developing the Nectar system [3] at Carnegie Mellon since 1987. The Nectar system is a high-bandwidth, low-latency computer network for connecting high-performance hosts. Hosts are attached using powerful network coprocessors (CABs) that accelerate communication protocols. Therefore for Nectar a node is a CAB-host pair. The Nectar network (Nectar-Net) consists of fiber-optic links and crossbar switches (HUBs). The network supports circuit switching, packet switching, multi-hop routing, and multicast communication. Figure 6 gives an overview of the Nectar system.

3.2.1 Nectar Prototype

We have developed a 26-node *Nectar prototype* system to support early system software and applications development. The prototype uses 100 Mb/s fiber links and 16×16 HUBs. The CAB is implemented as a separate board on the host VME backplane (see Figure 7). Via its VME bus interface, the CAB can connect to its host and to other devices such as graphics boards. Each CAB has 1 megabyte of data memory, 512 kilobytes of program memory, and a CPU based on a 20 MHz SPARC processor.

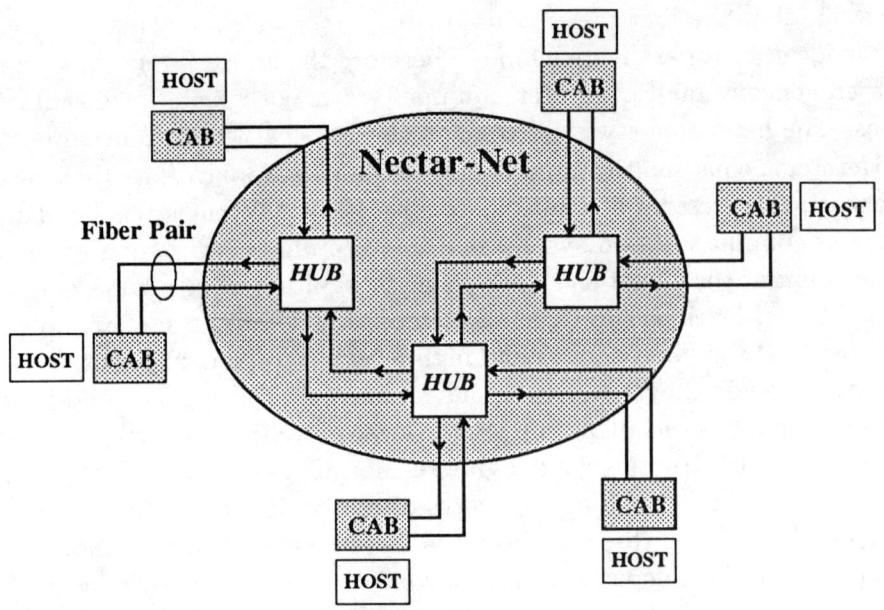

Figure 6:
Nectar system at Carnegie Mellon.

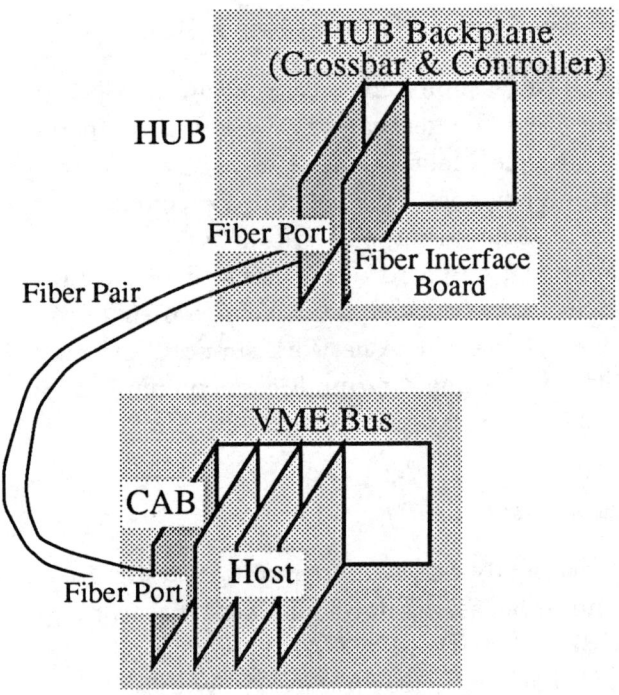

Figure 7:
HUB and CAB in Nectar prototype.

The CAB is connected to a HUB via a Fiber Port. For each direction (input or output), the Fiber Port contains the optoelectronics interface to a fiber line and a 4 kilobyte FIFO to buffer data and commands transferred over the fiber. The fiber port can support data rates up to 100 Mb/s. The CAB has a DMA controller to provide high speed transfers between the Fiber Port and the data memory, and between the data memory and the VME interface.

3.2.2 Nectar Systems Software

Using the Nectar prototype, we have developed an extensive set of software for the Nectar system. The CAB run-time system manages hardware devices such as timers and DMA, supports multiprogramming (the threads package [10]), and manages buffers (the mailbox module). The threads package, derived from the Mach C Threads package, supports lightweight processes in a single address space. Threads provide a low cost method of sharing the CAB CPU between concurrent activities, which is important for communication protocol implementation. Mailboxes provide efficient management of buffer space in the CAB memory and form the endpoints of communication between processes on hosts or CABs. Mailboxes also provide synchronization between readers and writers. For example, if a host process or CAB thread tries to read a message from an empty mailbox, it will block; it will resume automatically when a message is placed in the mailbox, typically by a transport-layer software on the CAB.

The streamlined structure of the CAB software has made it possible for Nectar to achieve the goal of low communication latency. For the existing Nectar prototype, the latency is under 1 microsecond to establish a connection through a single HUB; under 100 microseconds for a message sent between processes on separate CABs; and under 175 microseconds between processes residing in separate workstation hosts. (The transmission latency over a fiber depends on the length of the fiber; the above figures do not include the fiber latency.)

The Nectar prototype achieves the low-latency inter-host communication in two ways. First, network interrupt handling and transport protocol processing are off-loaded from the host to the CAB, whose hardware and software are specifically designed for protocol processing. This increases communication performance and also frees up the host for application processing. Second, by directly manipulating buffers in CAB memory, host processes can bypass the host operating system when reading and writing messages. By doing this, host processes avoid the cost of system calls and of data copying between the host process and the host operating system.

In the area of protocol software, the CAB currently supports several transport protocols with different reliability/overhead trade-offs [11]. The

CAB implementation of Internet standard protocols such as TCP/IP is also available. The TCP/IP throughput between two CABs is over 90 Mb/s for 16 kilobyte or larger packets, if the TCP checksum is turned off. Therefore high throughput TCP/IP implementation can be expected on the next-generation Nectar where the TCP checksum will be implemented in hardware.

3.2.3 Gigabit Nectar

To further develop the Nectar technology, Carnegie Mellon is working with Network Systems Corporation to develop a *gigabit Nectar* system capable of sustaining 1 Gb/s or higher speed end-to-end communication. This system is scheduled to be operational in 1992.

3.3 Advantages of Heterogeneous Multicomputers

Heterogeneous multicomputers such as Nectar offer substantial advantages in high-performance computing. The following summarizes some of these advantages [20]:

1. *Architectures matched to applications.* A heterogeneous multicomputer can incorporate nodes specially selected to suit a given application. Furthermore, a user or a piece of software can choose systems with proper architectures from existing nodes to process different parts of the application. Thus, instead of fitting computations of different characteristics to a single architecture as in the case of using conventional computer systems, heterogeneous multicomputers support a new computation paradigm that matches architectures to different computational needs. Therefore performance gains can be obtained through optimal use of architectures by the application.

2. *Cooperative and simultaneous use of heterogeneous architectures.* Heterogeneous nodes in the multicomputer can collaboratively work on the same application at the same time. Concurrency of various levels and of different grain sizes can be exploited simultaneously. This is made feasible by high-bandwidth and low-latency networks. It can be shown that heterogeneous multicomputers based on these networks can sustain the communication bandwidth required by nodes operating at high speed and allow concurrent processing of small-grain computations at different nodes [20].

3. *High-speed I/O.* The underlying high-speed network of a heterogeneous multicomputer is inherently suited to support high-speed I/O to devices such as displays, monitoring stations, sensors, file systems, mass stores and interfaces to other networks. These I/O devices can be viewed as special-purpose nodes of the multicomputer. High-speed

networks provide a key technology to speed up all these I/O devices substantially. For example, via such a network, disk arrays [17,12] can deliver very high data transfer rates to applications. With this and the capability of incorporating powerful computing nodes to fit application needs, heterogeneous multicomputers represent a balanced architectural approach capable of speeding up both computation and I/O in the same framework.

4. *Large memory accessible over network.* Over the underlying network of a heterogeneous multicomputer, applications can access a large amount of memory available in all the nodes. By combining memories from different nodes, one can address memory-bound problems such as logic simulation of very large circuits. For example, we have ported the COSMOS simulator [8] onto the Nectar prototype to handle large circuits that are too large to be simulated on a single node. Being able to address problems of large sizes, applications have the opportunity to benefit fully from the computation and I/O capabilities of a heterogeneous multicomputer.

5. *Use of existing architectures.* By incorporating systems of existing architectures as nodes, a heterogeneous multicomputer can take advantage of rapid improvements of commercially available computers. In addition, it can use systems software and applications that are already in place with these existing computers. For example, at Carnegie Mellon we have been able to port a large solid modeling application (developed by the NSF-sponsored Engineering Design Research Center on the campus) onto the Nectar prototype with a little effort. The porting was facilitated greatly by using as nodes those workstations on which the application had previously been developed.

6. *Incremental migration to new architectures.* A heterogeneous multicomputer provides a graceful environment for moving applications to new architectures such as special-purpose, parallel systems. That is, in the beginning an application can run only part of the computation on these new systems while using more conventional systems in the multicomputer to run the rest of the application. Thus the application can start using the new systems without having to move completely at once to the new environment. The application can increase its use of the new systems over time when more software and application code for the new environment is developed.

In summary, heterogeneous multicomputers offer a complete and balanced approach to high-performance computing. It provides powerful computing resources matched to applications needs. It can speed up both computation and I/O, and provide a large amount of memory. Moreover, it

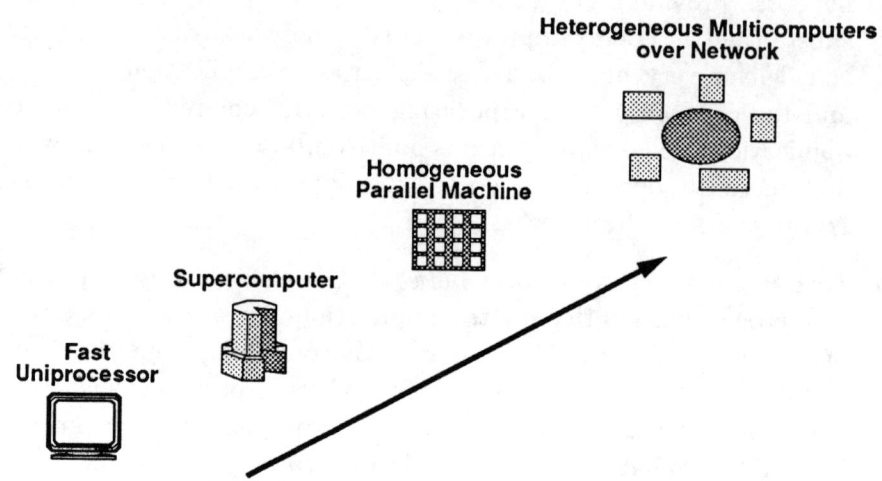

Figure 8:
Evolution of high-performance computing systems.

can take advantage of advances and infrastructures of existing architectures, while providing a graceful way of migrating the computing environment and applications to incorporate new architectures.

4 Concluding Remarks

Figure 8 depicts the evolution of high-performance computing systems. Starting from fast uniprocessors, it has proceeded to supercomputers, homogeneous parallel machines, and heterogeneous multicomputers.

Homogeneous parallel machines include shared memory multiprocessors and distributed memory parallel computers such as those cited in Section 1. With advances such as iWarp, these machines can now use highly integrated processors that have been specially designed to support fast and flexible interprocessor communication needed in parallel processing. This will substantially improve the performance of these systems and ease their programming.

To achieve the next level of performance, heterogeneous multicomputers will be needed to explore multiple levels and forms of parallelism, and allow heterogeneous processing nodes whenever appropriate. Heterogeneous systems are being pursued today in many high-performance computing installations for reasons including the above ones. It is important, however, that this is not done in an ad-hoc manner. We need to develop general and uniform hardware and software systems to incorporate different types of systems into the environment. The Nectar system has shown a general approach for constructing heterogeneous multicomputers.

Heterogeneous computing systems based on high-speed networks such as Nectar are redefining high-performance computing systems. Instead of building a single general-purpose computer for all computations, the emphasis is now placed on connecting together a variety of machines each with a unique strength in some area of computation. This new trend allows the use of the best architectures to meet individual application needs. As a result, these new heterogeneous systems can potentially solve some outstanding "grand-challenge" computation problems such as real-time weather prediction. We expect that rapid progress will be made in these areas and that an exciting new era of high-performance computing induced by heterogeneous multicomputers will unveil in the near future.

References

[1] Annaratone et al. Applications and algorithm partitioning on warp. In *COMPCON Spring '87*, pages 272–275. IEEE Computer Society, 1987.

[2] Annaratone et al. The warp computer: Architecture, implementation, and performance. *IEEE Transactions on Computers*, C-36(12):1523–1538, December 1987.

[3] Arnould et al. The design of nectar: A network backplane for heterogeneous multicomputers. In *Proceedings of Third International Conference on Architectural Support for Programming Languages and Operating Systems (ASPLOS III)*, pages 205–216. ACM, April 1989.

[4] W. C. Athas and C. L. Seitz. Multicomputers: Message-passing concurrent computers. *Computer*, 21(8):9–24, August 1988.

[5] Baxter et al. Building blocks for a new generation of application-specific computing systems. In *Proceedings of IEEE Application Specific Array Processor Conference*, Princeton, New Jersey, September 1990. IEEE.

[6] Borkar et al. iwarp: An integrated solution to high-speed parallel computing. In *Proceedings of Supercomputing '88*, pages 330–339, Orlando, Florida, November 1988. IEEE Computer Society and ACM SIGARCH.

[7] Borkar et al. Integrating systolic and memory communication in iwarp. In *Conference Proceedings of the 17th Annual International Symposium on Computer Architecture*, pages 70–81, May 1990.

[8] R. E. Bryant, D. Beatty, K. Brace, K. Cho, and T. Sheffler. Cosmos: A compiled simulator for mos circuits. In *Proceedings of the 24th Design Automation Conference*, pages 9–16. ACM/IEEE, June 1987.

[9] R. Cohn, T. Gross, M. Lam, and P. S. Tseng. Architecture and compiler tradeoffs for a long instruction word microprocessor. In *Proceedings of Third International Conference on Architectural Support for Programming Languages and Operating Systems (ASPLOS III)*, pages 2–14. ACM, April 1989.

[10] E. C. Cooper and R. P. Draves. C threads. Technical Report CMU-CS-88-154, Carnegie-Mellon University, Computer Science Department, June 1988.

[11] E. C. Cooper, P. A. Steenkiste, R. D. Sansom, and B. D. Zill. Protocol implementation on the nectar communication processor. In *Proceedings of the SIGCOMM '90 Symposium on Communications Architectures and Protocols*, Philadelphia, September 1990. ACM.

[12] D. A. Patterson, G. A. Gibson, and R. H. Katz. A case for redundant arrays of inexpensive disks (raid). In *Proceedings of ACM SIGMOD International Conference on Management of Data*, pages 109–116, June 1988.

[13] W. J. Dally and C. L. Seitz. The torus routing chip. *Distributed Computing*, 1(4):187–196, 1986.

[14] William J. Dally. *A VLSI Architecture for Concurrent Data Structures*. Kluwer Academic Publishers, 1987.

[15] L. G. C. Hamey, J. A. Webb, and I. C. Wu. *Low-level Vision on Warp and the Apply Programming Model*, pages 185–199. Kluwer Academic Publishers, 1987. Edited by J. Kowalik.

[16] M. Homewood et al. The ims t800 transputer. *IEEE Micro*, 7(5):10–26, October 1987.

[17] Katz et al. A project on high performance i/o subsystems. *ACM Computer Architecture News*, 17(17):24–31, 1989.

[18] H. T. Kung. Systolic communication. In *Proceedings of the International Conference on Systolic Arrays*, pages 695–703, San Diego, California, May 1988.

[19] H. T. Kung. Network-based multicomputers: Redefining high performance computing in the 1990s. In *Proceedings of Decennial Caltech Conference on VLSI*, pages 49–66, Pasadena, California, March 1989. MIT Press.

[20] H. T. Kung. Heterogeneous multicomputers. In R. F. Rashid, editor, *Carnegie Mellon Computer Science: A 25-Year Commemorative*, Reading, Massachusetts, 1990. Addison-Wesley.

[21] H. T. Kung and C. E. Leiserson. Systolic arrays (for vlsi). In *Sparse Matrix Proceedings 1978*, pages 256–282. SIAM, 1979. A slightly different version appears in *Introduction to VLSI Systems* by C. A. Mead and L. A. Conway, Addison-Wesley, 1980, Section 8.3, pp. 37-46.

[22] H. T. Kung. Why systolic architectures? *Computer Magazine*, 15(1):37–46, January 1982.

[23] H. T. Kung. Memory requirements for balanced computer architectures. *Journal of Complexity*, 1(1):147–157, 1985. (A revised version also appears in *Conference Proceedings of the 13th Annual International Symposium on Computer Architecture*, June 1986, pp. 49-54).

[24] M. Lam. *A Systolic Array Optimizing Compiler*. PhD thesis, Carnegie Mellon University, May 1987. The thesis is published by Kluwer Academic Publishers, Boston, Massachusetts, 1988.

[25] O. Menzilcioglu, H. T. Kung, and S. W. Song. Comprehensive evaluation of a two-dimensional configurable array. In *Proceedings of the Nineteenth International Symposium on Fault-Tolerant Computing*, pages 93–100. IEEE, 1989.

[26] Seitz et al. The architecture and programming of the ametek series 2010 multicomputer. In *The Third Confererence on Hypercube Concurrent Computers and Applications*, pages 33–36, Pasadena, California, January 1988.

[27] C. L. Seitz. The cosmic cube. *Communications of the ACM*, 28(1):22–33, January 1985.

[28] L. W. Tucker and G. G. Robertson. Architecture and applications of the connection machine. *Computer Magazine*, 21(8):26–38, August 1988.

Chapter 2
Optical Interconnections in Computing

Joseph W. Goodman[*]

1 Introduction

Rapid advances in integrated circuit technology have resulted in dramatic increases in gate speeds and circuit densities. It is generally agreed that the technology has now passed the phase in which chip speeds can be greatly improved by further advances in gate speed, and entered the phase in which speed is limited by interconnections between gates or between groups of gates [1]. Interest is high in new interconnect technologies that may remove some of the limitations of traditional metal interconnects, with particular attention being paid to optical interconnects and superconducting electrical interconnects. This paper addresses some issues in the area of optical interconnect technology. In particular, it considers some of the potential advantages of optics, it discusses some past uses of optics for this purpose, and it outlines some of the difficulties that are currently encountered in trying to apply such a technology at various levels of the interconnect hierarchy.

2 The Interconnect Hierarchy

Problems are encountered at many levels of a hierarchy of interconnects in computing. We exclude from consideration here the problem of interconnecting different machines (a problem to which optics is already providing unique contributions) and focus instead on intracomputer interconnections within a single machine. At the highest level, functional modules must be interconnected to other functional modules, where a functional module might be a processor or a memory unit in a multiprocessor machine. At the next level, it is necessary to interconnect different backplanes in a machine, where a backplane is the physical entity into which electronic boards are inserted and through which they communicate. Stepping down another level, electronic boards must communicate with other boards through a backplane.

---

[*]Department of Electrical Engineering, Stanford University, Stanford, California 94305.

On a single board, multichip carriers must communicate with other multichip carriers. On a multichip carrier, chips must communicate with other chips. At the lowest level of the hierarchy, gates must communicate with other gates on a single chip.

The interconnect requirements at each of these levels are in general different, in terms of the typical length of the interconnect (as much as a few meters at the module-to-module level and no more than a few millimeters at the gate-to-gate level) and in terms of the data rate (for example, as low as a few Mb/s at the gate-to-gate level to greater than 10 Gb/s at the backplane level). The application of optics to solving an interconnect problem is usually easiest at the highest levels of the hierarchy and most difficult at the lowest levels, for reasons that will be apparent later.

3 Desirable Attributes of Optics as an Interconnect Technology

The most important fundamental advantage of optics as an interconnect technology comes from the lack of interaction of incoherent optical beams in a linear medium [6,7]. This property implies that there is no fundamental mechanism by which crosstalk and mutual interference are generated, at least at power levels that are small enough to assure linearity. Of course there are practical effects that can result in crosstalk, such as scattering of light at imperfect surfaces, but the very fact that these effects are not fundamental implies that with sufficient care they can be made insignificant. This property of photons should be contrasted with that of electrons, which, as moving charged particles, do interact through mechanisms as fundamental as those described by Maxwell's equations. It is often necessary to take extraordinary precautions to assure that nearby electrical signals do not interact.

As a corollary, the very property of photons that makes them attractive as an interconnect technology would appear to make them unattractive in a gate technology. In a logic gate we require that two signals interact nonlinearly to produce a third signal. Such interactions are relatively easy to achieve with electrical signals, but more difficult to achieve optically. In fact, nonlinear interaction of optical beams would seem to always be generated by electronic effects on the atomic or molecular scale.

A second advantage of optics as an interconnect technology is found when considering the need to terminate interconnections with their characteristic impedance. When the data rate and length of the interconnect are such that it behaves as a transmission line, proper termination of the line becomes an important issue. If the line is not terminated in its characteristic impedance, reflections from the end will occur, and these reflections will eventually return to corrupt the transmitted signal and cause logic errors. Optical beams traveling in fibers also reflect from the glass/air interface at the end of the fiber, so what is the difference between the two cases? An answer comes only when we consider the fact that construction of a proper terminating impedance becomes more and more difficult when the fractional bandwidth (bandwidth/carrier frequency) becomes large. The termination must have the prescribed impedance at all frequencies contained within the transmitted signal. Consider a data signal at 1 Gb/s transmitted electrically as a baseband signal. The fractional bandwidth is at least unity (possibly greater than unity, depending on the exact definition of fractional bandwidth) in this case. On the other hand, consider the same 1 Gb/s signal modulated as an intensity modulation on an optical carrier. The fractional bandwidth of this signal is tiny (of the order of 10^{-5}) and therefore a termination (in this case a multilayer coating) that works over the entire bandwidth is fundamentally easier to achieve than in the electrical case.

A second case in which reflections are important comes at branching points where fan out takes place. Electrical lines with large fan out tend to have significant problems with reflections. Such reflections are fundamentally easier to control with optical signals, again due to the smaller fractional bandwidth.

A third potential advantage of optics comes from considerations of the electrical power required to establish an interconnect of a given length and at a given data rate. We will later point out that *in certain cases* an optical interconnect will require less power than an electrical interconnect. However, this is by no means a universal rule.

Finally, optical interconnects have a certain freedom from planar and quasi-planar constraints not shared by electrical interconnects. In the electrical case, it is important to remain near a ground plane, so that fields from one interconnect line will terminate on the ground plane, rather than on adjacent interconnect lines (thus causing crosstalk). No such requirement exists in the optical case. Due to the very short wavelength, optical signals can be very well confined, whether in dielectric waveguides such as fibers or in free space beams.

4 Differences Between Long Distance Communications and Intracomputer Communication

It is important to distinguish between the problems of long distance communication and those of intracomputer communications. In the long distance case, attenuation, modal dispersion and material dispersion are all phenomena of the greatest consequence, for they limit the length-bandwidth product that can be achieved. For these reasons long distance optical communication is dominated by single mode, rather than multimode, fiber. In addition, 1.3 microns and 1.55 microns are the wavelengths of choice, where material dispersion and attenuation are minimal. Finally, the cost of single-mode fiber dominates the cost of a very long link (e.g. 100 km), and therefore it is most economical to multiplex as much information as possible into a single ultra-high-speed channel, rather than using several parallel optical channels on different fibers, each running at a lower speed.

Most of the above requirements are missing in the intracomputer communication problem. Material dispersion is generally not important when the distances involved are just a few meters at most, with the result that 0.8 microns wavelength may be quite acceptable (the choice of wavelength will probably be made on the basis of *reliability*). Attenuation is not important if fibers are used, although it can be important if waveguides are used on a large board (e.g. an attenuation of 0.5 dB per cm over 1 m could be problematic). Modal dispersion is not significant in many local communication problems, and multimode technology is often simpler and less costly than single-mode technology. Finally, for such short distances, the cost of the optical fiber (if one is used) is a small part of the overall cost, and multichannel solutions running at low data rates could conceivably be preferred in some cases, depending on the cost and area occupied by the interfaces.

Thus the different physical constraints present in the intracomputer communication problem suggest that the traditional solutions of long distance communication may not be the best solutions in this type of problem.

5 Examples of Uses of Optics in Solving Intracomputer Interconnect Problems

The field of interconnects is still at a young age, but several examples of the use of optical interconnects within computers already exist. Perhaps the best known and the oldest is the use of optical fiber to connect backplanes in the 5-ESS switching computers made by AT&T. According to sources within AT&T, the reason for use of optics was not to provide ultra-high-speed links between the backplanes, but rather to electrically isolate them and thereby to prevent ground loops.

A second example of the use of optics is the Dialog.H computer built by the Electrotechnical Laboratory in Tsukuba, Japan [19]. This machine contains several processors, each with their own local memory. The processors communicate with each other through a time-shared optical channel. Each processor contains a high-speed laser diode and a fast photodetector. The laser diodes broadcast light through free space to a cylindrical mirror, which spreads the light across the optical receivers of all the processors. Optical headers on the messages identify their destinations. In this way a time-shared network between processors is realized.

A new example has recently been reported by the NTT Transmission Systems Laboratory [15], the so-called COSINE-I system. This system consists of 36 processors (T800 transputers), each with 1 Mbyte of local memory and each on a separate board. Each transputer has four communication ports running at 20 Mbits/sec per port. The 36 boards are interconnected optically through free space. Currently, reconfiguration of the interconnects is done manually, but a future version of the system will use an optical crossbar switch.

The three above examples use optics for interconnects at the backplane-to-backplane level, the functional-module-to-functional-module level, and the board-to-board level, respectively. Considerable additional work is in progress at lower levels of the hierarchy.

6 Research at Lower Levels of the Interconnect Hierarchy

There are a great many research efforts around the world exploring the possible use of optics for interconnections at lower levels of the interconnect hierarchy. Several groups have been exploring the use of holographic interconnects [10,11,4,5,14]. Optical clock distribution at the chip level has been studied for silicon chips [2,3]. A photonic backplane has been constructed for an experimental switching computer [9]. Optical interconnects have been investigated for possible use in the Connection Machine [12]. Much of the work on Optoelectronic Integrated Circuits (OEIC's) and Photonic Integrated Circuits (PIC's) is relevant to interconnections at many levels of the hierarchy.

An interesting project on optical interconnects has been initiated in Europe as part of ESPRIT-II program [17]. The title of the project is OLIVES, which is an abbreviation for OpticaL Interconnections for VIsi and Electronic Systems. Ten organizations are participating in the program, including five academic institutions and five industrial groups. The total level of effort is approximately 60 man years, spread over three years. The goal of the project is to investigate backplane, board and chip level interconnects for advanced processor systems. The approach under investigation at the backplane level involves the use of a so-called "optical mastercard," which is a highly multi-moded planar optical channel that conducts light between electronic boards. Another effort is aimed at realizing an optical clock distribution system at the level of a multichip carrier. Considerable effort is also being devoted to suitable device technology.

7 Power Considerations

The power required to realize an interconnect is an extremely important parameter. If the power required for one technology is significantly greater than that required for another, the latter may well be the solution of choice. Thus it is important to understand the power requirements of both electrical and optical interconnects.

Studies of power requirements have been reported [10]. We present here only the results and extract conclusions from them. In all cases the assumption is that we wish to realize a 1 Gb/s interconnect and that the interconnect must charge a gate capacitance at the far end to a threshold voltage of 1 volt. For the electrical case we have assumed a silicon chip with 0.5 micron linewidth. The results are as follows:

	Required Power
Electrical Case	
Gate to gate interconnect	
(silicon chip, 0.5 micron line width, 1 mm distance)	35 mW
Chip to chip interconnect	
(RC interconnect, 25 micron square bonding pads)	1 mW
Chip to chip interconnect	
(lossless transmission line, 50 ohm termination)	10 mW
Optical Case	
Laser source	
(25% source efficiency, 1 mA threshold)	2 mW

Communication Power Requirements

The optical result holds for all optical interconnects, regardless of their level in the hierarchy.

The results indicate that at the gate to gate level, unless extremely low threshold lasers are developed, there is relatively little reason to use optics at this level. The electrical solution seems far superior. The first chip-to-chip example is one in which the problem is dominated by the bonding pad capacitances; a full mW of power is required. The second chip-to-chip example utilizes a terminated transmission line. It is extremely important to note the great escalation of power (10 mW) required that occurs when the line must be terminated. The optical solution requires an electrical power essentially similar to that needed for the RC interconnect between chips—considerably less than that required for the terminated electrical line.

The potential advantages of optics with respect to communication energy required per bit (or for a fixed data rate, average power) have been examined in a more fundamental context in [16]. There it is shown that an optical interconnect can be viewed as providing an impedance transformation. Unfortunately, Nature has left us with rather low characteristic impedances for electrical transmission lines. Since the power required by an interconnect is V^2/R_0, where V is the threshold voltage and R_0 is the characteristic impedance, low characteristic impedance implies high average power or high energy per bit. An optical interconnect can in principle supply an interconnect in which a high impedance level is present in both the source and detector circuitry, while transmission takes place through a fiber, waveguide, or free space, where the characteristic impedance is considerably lower (the characteristic impedance of free space is only 377 ohms).

8 Problems Encountered with Optical Interconnects

Each interconnect technology has its own set of characteristic problems. Optical interconnects are no exception. We address these problems here with the goal of assessing which ones are the most serious.

The first problem of importance concerns photonic device reliability [18], and in particular the reliability of optical sources. Light emitting diodes are very reliable, but also suffer from low efficiency (at best a few percent) of conversion of electrical power into optical power. Laser diodes are far more efficient (20% to 25% for communication grade sources) and therefore of greater interest for optical interconnections. Current reliability estimates for laser diodes are of the order of 10^6 hours (about 100 years) MTBF. While 100 years seems to be a respectable lifetime, it may nonetheless be the factor that determines how far down the interconnect hierarchy optics can penetrate. If we take 1 year MTBF somewhat arbitrarily as our system goal, then no interconnect application requiring more than 100 laser diodes in the system will be acceptable from the point of view of reliability. This limit would prevent the use of optics for chip to chip communication in many systems, unless optics were limited to only a few of the more critical interconnects. It certainly would rule out optics at the gate-to-gate level. It may be preferable to use modulators, rather than sources, on chip, and to use a small number of high-power lasers off chip to provide the optical power. The reliability of modulators should be greater than that of sources, so a net improvement of MTBF could be achieved.

A second problem to be mentioned is that of laser threshold currents. The most common laser diodes have thresholds in the tens to hundreds of milliamps range, and as such require a considerable minimum commitment to power to establish an interconnect (unless off-chip lasers are used to supply the optical power for many interconnects, as suggested above). For the past few years dramatic improvements in laser threshold currents have been reported. Sub-milliamp thresholds have been reported by several research groups (e.g. [13]), even for vertically emitting laser diodes [8]. Further improvements are still possible and can be expected in the next few years. Reduction of the threshold current of lasers is critical to the success of optical interconnect technology, particularly at all but the highest levels of the interconnect hierarchy.

A third problem comes from the rather short distances involved in the interconnections of interest. While we have argued that it is fundamentally easier to provide impedance-matching terminations at optical frequencies than at electrical frequencies for a given modulation bandwidth, nonetheless the quality of the terminations may have to be very good indeed. Even small amounts of light reflected back into the laser source can cause significant intensity noise to appear on the laser output. Thus while achieving sufficiently broad terminations may not be a problem, achieving sufficiently well-matched terminations may be. The short communication distances do not yield any appreciable waveguide attenuation of the reflections on their way back to the source.

A fourth problem of concern may be modal noise. Since multimode solutions are of great interest for short interconnections, one cannot help but worry as to whether the typical intensity-dependent frequency modulation of laser sources may lead to unacceptable modal noise at the interconnect output. However, this may not be as much of a problem as might be supposed at the start. Modal noise diminishes as a problem when the number of modes involved becomes very large. Thus as long as the modal volume intercepted by all detectors can be kept large enough to contain many modes, noise problems should be minimized.

A final problem worth mentioning is physical area required by the electrical-to-optical and optical-to-electrical interfaces required at the ends of optical interconnects. If the area devoted to these conversions is too large, the lower levels of the interconnect hierarchy may not be reachable by this technology. In this regard the attenuation of the optical interconnects may become an important consideration, for high attenuation implies the need for amplification, which in turn requires area.

9 Concluding Remarks

Optical technology has had a profound impact on the field of communications. It is beginning to have a similar impact on the field of computing. The role of fiber optics in machine-to-machine communication is indisputably important. We are now seeing the beginnings of a push to bring optics within individual machines. The critical intellectual question at the moment is how far down the interconnect hierarchy optics can penetrate. The answer to this question is heavily dependent on progress in device technology, as well as on the conception of innovative optical approaches to solving these problems. At this point in time, a reasonable guess at the answer might be that optics will gradually invade those interconnect problems where the electrical solution requires a terminating impedance. In such problems, optics can provide a solution that is very competitive in terms of power requirements.

References

[1] H. B. Bakoglu, *Circuits, Interconnections, and Packaging for VLSI*, Addison Wesley (1990).

[2] B. D. Clymer, J. W. Goodman, "Optical clock distribution to silicon chips," *Opt. Engin.*, **25**, 1103-1108 (1986).

[3] B. D. Clymer, J. W. Goodman, "Timing uncertainty for receivers in optical clock distribution for VLSI," *Opt. Engin.*, **27**, 944-954 (1988).

[4] M. R. Feldman, C. C. Guest, "Computer generated holographic optical elements for optical interconnection of very large scale integrated circuits," *Appl. Opt.*, **26**, 4377 (1987).

[5] M. R. Feldman, C. C. Guest, "Holograms for optical interconnects for VLSI circuits fabricated by electron-beam holography," *Opt. Engin.*, **28**, 915-921 (1989).

[6] J. W. Goodman, F. J. Leonberger, S. -Y. Kung, R. A. Athale, "Optical interconnections for VLSI systems," *Proc. IEEE*, **72**, No. 7, 850-866 (1984).

[7] J. W. Goodman, "Optics as an Interconnect Technology," in *Optical Processing and Computing*, H.H. Arsenault, Ed., Academic Press, 1-32 (1989).

[8] J. L. Jewell, Y. H. Lee, A. Scherer, S. L. McCall, N. A. Olsson, J. P. Harbison, L. T. Florez, "Surface-emitting microlasers for photonic switching and interchip connections," *Opt. Engin.*, **29**, 210-214 (1990).

[9] D. A. Kahn, E. A. Munter, M. R. Wernik, "A photonic backplane for a high capacity time switch," *Proc. of the International Switching Symposium*, C7.4.1-C7.4.5, IEEE CH2431-5/87/0000-0587 (1987).

[10] R. K. Kostuk, J. W. Goodman, "Optical imaging applied to microelectronic chip-to-chip interconnections," *Appl. Opt.*, **24**, 2851-2858 (1984).

[11] R. K. Kostuk, Y-T. Huang, D. Heterington, M. Kato, "Reducing alignment and chromatic sensitivity of holographic optical interconnects with substrate mode holograms," *Appl. Opt.*, **28**, 4939-4944 (1989).

[12] T. A. Lane, J. A. Quam, B. O. Kahle, E. C. Parish, "Gigabit optical interconnects for the connection machine," *Proc. SPIE*, **1178**, 24-35 (1990).

[13] K. Lau, P. L. Derry, A. Yariv, "Ultimate limit in low threshold quantum well GaAlAs semiconductor lasers," *Appl. Phys. Let.*, **52**, 88-90 (1988).

[14] F. Lin, E. M. Strelecki, T. Jannson, "Optical multiplanar VLSI interconnects based on multiplexed waveguide holograms," *Appl. Optics*, **29**, 1126-1133 (1990).

[15] T. Matsumoto, T. Sakano, K. Noguchi, T. Sawabe, "A parallel-processing computer system employing reconfigurable board-to-board free space optical interconnections: COSINE-1," *Proc. of the International Optical Computing Conference*, Kobe Japan, 1990.

[16] D. A. B. Miller, "Optics for low-energy communication inside digital processors: quantum detectors, sources, and modulators as efficient impedance converters," *Optics Let.*, **14**, 146-148 (1989).

[17] J. W. Parker, "ESPRIT II OLIVES—A European collaborative program in optical interconnections," *Proc. of the International Optical Computing Conference*, Kobe, Japan, 1990.

[18] P. W. Shumate, "Reliability considerations for optoelectronic interconnections," *Proc. SPIE*, **703**, 96-99 (1986).

[19] H. Tajima, Y. Okada, K. Tamura, "A high-speed optical common bus for a multiprocessor system," *Trans. Inst. Electron. and Commun. Eng. Japan*, **24**, No. 17, 850-866 (1984).

Chapter 3
A View of Computational Learning Theory*

Leslie G. Valiant[†]

1 Introduction

At present computers are programmed by an external agent, a human, who presents an explicit description of the algorithm to be executed to the machine. There would be clear advantages in having machines that could learn, in the sense that they could acquire knowledge by means other than explicit programming. It is not self-evident that machine learning is feasible at all. The existence of biological systems that perform learning apparently as a result of computations in their nervous systems provides, however, a strong plausibility argument in its favor.

When contrasted with currently understood methods of knowledge acquisition, learning as exhibited by humans, and even so-called lower animals, is a spectacular phenomenon. What is the nature of this phenomenon? What are the laws and limitations governing it?

Although the engineering of learning systems and the understanding of human learning are both very relevant we place at the center of our investigations a third point of view, namely that of seeking to understand for its own sake the computational phenomenon of learning. Understanding the ultimate possibilities may be more fruitful in the long run then either of the other two approaches, and may even turn out to be easier. As an analogy one can consider the question of understanding motion in physics. The engineering of moving vehicles and the understanding of human movement both raise interesting and challenging questions. The more general question of understanding the laws and limitations of motion itself, however, has yielded the more fundamental insights.

In general usage the word learning has a great variety of senses. Our aim here is to discuss just one of these, namely inductive learning, which we consider to be both central and amenable to analysis. Induction has been

---

*Research at Harvard was supported by the National Science Foundation NSF-CCR-89-02500, the Office for Naval Research ONR-N0014-85-K-0445, the Center for Intelligent Control ARO DAAL 03-86-K-0171 and by DARPA AFOSR 89-0506.

[†]Harvard University and NEC Research Institute.

investigated extensively by philosophers and its nature debated. It has to do with the phenomenon of successful generalization. Humans appear to be able to abstract from experience principles that are not strictly implied in the experience. For example, after seeing relatively few classified examples of a category, such as that of a chair, a child is able to classify further natural examples with remarkable and mysterious accuracy.

The centrality of induction has been recognized from the beginning. According to Aristotle "all belief comes from either syllogism or induction." Its nature has proved more elusive. Hume's view, that regularities in experience give rise to habits in expectation, seems to capture the essence of induction. It does not make explicit, however, the specific nature of the regularities that give rise to such habits. It seems clear that these regularities must have some particular nature, which is another way of saying that for generalization to work some assumptions have to be made. In the absence of any assumptions, a child after seeing some objects, all identified as chairs, would be unjustified in reaching any opinion whatever about unseen objects.

In [77] a theory was proposed in which Hume's regularities are not imposed by properties of the observed world, but by computational limitations internal to the learner. In particular the assumption underlying the induction process is that what is being learned can be learned by a computational process that is quantitatively feasible. This approach offers two philosophical advantages. First it makes no assumptions about the world, complex as it is. This is important since, in contrast with physics where many simple laws have been found, at the level of cognition and human concepts no analogous simple regularities have been identified. The second philosophical advantage is that the assumptions that are made can be argued to be self-evidently true. The concepts that humans do learn from examples are, by definition, learnable from examples. The assumptions, however, are not vacuous. For example, learnability implies that the programs learned have small representations, a restriction that reduces the set of possibilities to a minute subset of all possible functions. Current evidence suggests that the constraint of computational feasibility on the learning process restricts the class even further than this.

In this paper we review some of the recent results that relate to this one framework for studying learning. Our treatment is necessarily at best partial even for this one model and no attempt is made here to relate it to other approaches. Various reviews of related material can be found in [21,31,39,42,49]. Our aim is to give a brief view of these results. We make particular reference to questions such as the following: Which of the results are unexpected or surprising? What new insight have been gained? What range of learning phenomena can be usefully discussed in this framework? What new algorithms have been discovered? Learning appears to be a rich and diverse field and we are clearly a long way from having even the roughest outline of the possibilities.

2 A Model for Learning by Example

Our model can be viewed as a specification of the functional behavior desired of a mechanism that purports to do learning. In the simplest version it models the learning of a concept or function from positive and negative examples of it. We will discuss this version most extensively. The definition attempts, however, to capture learning at a broader level and, as we shall see, is adaptable to a variety of learning situations.

The model incorporates two basic notions. The first is that one cannot hope to perform inductive learning to perfection. Some level of error in what is learned is inevitable. The learner should be able to estimate an upper bound on the error at any stage of learning and should be able to control it. In particular, he should be able to make it arbitrarily small if he is willing to spend more resources such as time or the number of examples seen. To be specific we shall insist that the resources needed to reduce the error to ε should grow only as a fixed polynomial $p(1/\varepsilon)$.

The second basic notion is that in any theory of learning one should give an account of how the computations performed can be done in feasibly few steps. In particular, we shall require that the resources be again bounded by a fixed polynomial in the relevant parameters, such as the size of the minimal description of the program being learned, or the number of variables in the system.

As we shall see later there is evidence suggesting that the class of all programs is not learnable in the above sense. Hence learning algorithms will restrict themselves to some special class C of functions. Typically the algorithm computes a representation of some special form of the function, and the choice of this knowledge representation is often critical. Depending on the application area different styles of representation may be appropriate. For cognitive tasks one based on logic is natural. The simplest such representations are Boolean expressions. Where continuous variables are involved geometric criteria are more appropriate. Thus we may represent an example of a concept in n-dimensional space by a set of n coordinate values. A concept may be represented, for example, as a hyperplane that separates positive from negative examples. Lastly in linguistic contexts where sequences are important one may consider automata-theoretic characterizations.

In general we consider that the cognitively most relevant setting for learning is one in which the system already has much knowledge. The basic variables can then be either the primitive input variables of the system or the outputs of arbitrarily complex programs that are already part of the system (by virtue of preprogramming or previous learning). Thus learning is always relative to the existing knowledge base. This is important for two reasons. First, it implies that a theory of relative learning is sufficient. Second, it highlights an important advantage of learning over programming. It may be infeasible to augment the knowledge of a system by programming, even in a minor way, if the state of the system is so complex that it is difficult for the outside agent to understand it. In contrast, learning takes place relative to the current state since the program sought takes as inputs the outputs of whatever complex programs the system already contains.

We shall define our basic model as one for learning predicates (or concepts) from examples and counterexamples of it. The aim of the learning algorithm is to find a rule (or program or hypothesis) that reliably categorizes unseen examples as being positive or negative. Let X be the *domain* from which the examples are drawn. A *concept* $c \subseteq X$ is the set of positive examples. This is sometimes denoted by $pos(c)$, while its complement $X - pos(c)$ is denoted by $neg(c)$. It is meaningful to discuss the learnability of a class C of concepts rather than that of a single concept. For example, for Boolean functions over n variables we would define X to be $\{0,1\}^n$. An example of a Boolean concept class over $\{0,1\}^5$ would be the class of 2-disjunctive normal form expressions (2-DNF) consisting of all predicates that can be written as a disjunction of length two conjunctions. An example of an individual concept in this class would be that defined by the expression $x_1 x_3 + \bar{x}_2 x_3 + x_1 x_4 + \bar{x}_2 x_4$.

It turns out that it is sometimes important in the learning context to distinguish the functions being learned from particular representations of them. The learner needs to represent the hypothesis somehow and we shall denote the class of such representations by H. The above example is logically equivalent to the expression $(x_1 + \bar{x}_2)(x_3 + x_4)$, but the difficulty of learning some class containing this instance may be different. For brevity our notation will sometimes identify functions with their representation where this makes no difference. Learning by an efficiently universal class of representations, such as Boolean circuits, is sometimes called prediction [35].

In general we want to determine how fast the computational difficulty of learning increases as some size parameter $|c|$ of the concept grows. We shall therefore regard as stratified both the domain $X = \bigcup_{n \geq 1} X_n$ as well as the class of representations $C = \bigcup_{n \geq 1} C_n$. Typically n will be the number of variables. We can also introduce a further parameter s to define, for example, the size of a Boolean expression. Then $C_n = \bigcup_{s \geq 1} C_{n,s}$, where $C_{n,s}$ denotes the subclass of C consisting of concepts with parameters n and s.

We assume that for each $c \in C$ there are two probability distributions D^+ and D^- that describe the relative probability of occurrence in nature of the elements in $pos(c)$ and $neg(c)$ respectively. The distributions represent the nature of the world, about which we wish to make no assumptions. Hence they are allowed to be unknown and arbitrary except for time invariance.

Learning in a changing world is clearly more difficult. Analysis of that situation remains to be done.

If $c \in C$ is the concept being learned and $h \in H$ is the hypothesis of the learner, we define the error $e^+(h)$ to be the probability according to D^+ that a random $x \in pos(c)$ belongs to $neg(h)$. Analogously $e^-(h)$ is the probability according to D^- that a random $x \in neg(c)$ belongs to $pos(h)$.

We now define a class C to be *learnable* by representation class H, both over some domain X, if the following holds: There exists a learning algorithm A that for some polynomial p, for any $c \in C$, for any D^+, D^- and any $0 < \varepsilon, \delta < 1$, given access to random draws from D^+, D^- in any one step, will output in $p(1/\varepsilon, 1/\delta, |c|)$ steps a hypothesis h that with probability at least $1 - \delta$ will have

$$e^+(h) < \varepsilon \quad \text{and} \quad e^-(h) < \varepsilon$$

where $|c|$ is some agreed measure of concept complexity (e.g. number of variables plus size of description of c in bits.)

The definition finesses the issue of the distribution being unknown by requiring only that the hypothesis perform well on the same unknown distribution from which the examples are drawn. The requirement that the same algorithm perform well on a variety of distributions seems natural since in human learning one must presume that no more than a limited number of learning algorithms are being applied in a wide variety of contexts. Furthermore current analysis suggests that insistence on good performance even in worst-case distributions is not as onerous as worst-case requirements in some other areas of computation, such as graph algorithms, appear to be. For example, restricting to uniform distributions is not known to make many classes learnable that are not so otherwise.

If the computational requirement is removed from the definition then we are left with the notion of nonparametric inference in the sense of statistics, as discussed in particular by Vapnik [80]. For discrete domains all reasonable representations are then learnable [17]. What gives special flavor to our definition is the additional requirement of efficient computation. This appears to restrict the learnable classes very severely. This model has been described as "probably approximately correct" or *pac* learning [3]. Since the efficiency aspect is so central a more accurate acronym would be *epac* learning.

The quantitative requirement in the definition is that the runtime, and hence also the number of examples sought, has to be bounded by a fixed polynomial in $1/\varepsilon, 1/\delta$ as well as in the parameters that specify the complexity of the instance being learned. With doubly stratified classes such as $C_{n,s}$ both n the number of variables and s the size of the concept would be parameters.

The model is not restricted to discrete domains. Blumer et al. [18] describe a formulation allowing geometric concepts. For example in n-dimensional Euclidean space a natural concept class is that of a half-space [58]. In such domains one has to state how one charges for representing and operating on a real number. Typically charging one unit is appropriate for both cases.

In the definition as given, learning refers to the acquisition of new information, and the parameter optimised is the accuracy ε. Similar formulations are possible for other situations also. For example the learner may not be acquiring new information but may seek to increase some measure of performance at a task as a result of training.

3 Robustness of Model

For any computational model it is important to ask how it relates to alternative formalisms that attempt to capture similar intuitions. A series of recent results has established that the pac model is robust in the sense that the set of learnable classes remains invariant under a large range of variations in the definitions.

Several aspects of the definition contain some arbitrariness and it is natural to ask first whether the particular choices made make any difference. Haussler et al. [34] review some twenty-eight variations and show them all equivalent. One issue, for example, is whether the decision to have separate sources for positive and negative examples rather than a single source and distribution, enhances or diminishes the power of the model. It turns out that it makes no difference.

Among further variations shown to be equivalent in [34] are those generated by the choice of whether the parameters $\varepsilon, \delta, n, s$ are given as part of the input to the learning algorithm or not. Also, allowing the learning algorithm to be randomized rather than deterministic adds no power (under weak regularity assumptions on H) since any randomness needed can be extracted from the source of random examples. A further issue is the treatment of the confidence parameter δ. It does not make any difference whether we insist on the complexity to be bounded by a constant or a polynomial in $\log(1/\delta)$ rather than a polynomial in δ.

Haussler et al. [35] consider models where the examples are viewed as coming in a sequence. The algorithm, on seeing each example, makes a prediction about it, and on receiving the true classification updates itself if necessary. They define models where the total number of mistakes made is polynomial bounded, or the probability that a mistake is made at any one step diminishes appropriately. They show that these models are equivalent to the pac model if the representation is universal (e.g. Boolean circuits).

Two further variations are group learning and weak learning, both of which appear on the surface to be strictly less demanding models. In the first the requirement is to find a hypothesis that, when given a set of examples, of appropriate polynomial size, promised to be all positive or all negative, determines which is the case, as the pac model does for single examples. In the second, weak learning, we revert to classifying single examples again but are satisfied with accuracy $1/2 + 1/p$ when p is a polynomial in the relevant parameters. This captures the gambling context when it is sufficient to have any discernible odds in one's favor. That these two models are equivalent to each other was shown in [46,43]. Subsequently in a surprising development Schapire [73] gave a construction showing that they are equivalent to the pac model also. His construction shows that the accuracy of any learning algorithm can be boosted provided it works for all distributions. An alternative construction has been given recently by Freund [25].

The results above all give evidence of robustness with respect to changes in definition of the model. A second important but different robustness issue is that of whether learnability of classes is preserved under various simple mathematical operations on the classes or their members. It is shown in [41] that the learnability of a class is preserved under a wide class of substitutions of variables. It follows from this that learning most classes of Boolean formulae does not become easier if we forbid repetitions of variables or negations of variables. Pitt and Warmuth [65] consider much more general reductions that preserve learnability. They use it to show such unexpected relationships as that the learnability of finite automata would imply the learnability of Boolean formulae. Lastly we mention that the closure properties of learnable classes can be investigated for such operations as union, differences, nested differences and composition [41,36,61].

4 Some More Demanding Variants

4.1 Resilience to Errors

The model as described does not allow for any errors in the data. In a practical situation one would expect that examples would be occasionally misclassified or their description corrupted. Clearly it would be desirable to have algorithms that are resilient in the sense that they would generate hypotheses of acceptable accuracy even when errors occur in the examples at some rate.

Several models of error have been proposed. It is generally assumed that each example called is correct with probability $1 - \mu$ independent of previous examples. A worst-case, the so called malicious, model allows that with probability μ the example returned be arbitrary both as far as the description of the example as well as its classification. Both parts can be constructed by an adversary with full knowledge of the state of the learning algorithm. Even with this model a certain level of error can be tolerated for some classes of Boolean functions [78]. By very general arguments Kearns and Li [40] have shown, however, that the accuracy rate $(1-\varepsilon)$ cannot exceed $(1 - \mu/(1 - \mu))$.

If we disallow corruption of the data but allow the classification to be wrong with probability μ for each example independently, then learning becomes more tractable. Angluin and Laird [5] show for certain Boolean classes (k-CNF) that learning to arbitrarily small ε can be done for any known $\mu < 1/2$. Analyses of intermediate models are given by Shackelford and Volper [74] and by Sloan [76].

The issue of errors is clearly important. There are large gaps in our current knowledge even for simple representations such as conjunctions [40]. For geometric concepts in the case that the erroneous examples can be arbitrary even less is known. For example, there is no satisfactory algorithm or theory known for learning half-spaces with such errors.

4.2 Positive Examples Only

The question of whether humans learn largely from positive examples has received much attention. From a philosophical viewpoint induction from examples of just one kind appears even more paradoxical than the general case. It turns out, however, that such learning is feasible in some simple cases such as conjunctions and vector spaces [36,75,77]. Some general criteria for learning from positive only examples are given in [59].

Learning from examples of one kind has features that distinguish it from the general case. On the assumption that $P = NP$ the class of all Boolean circuits is learnable in the two-sided case. This is not true in the one-sided case. In fact, learning simple disjunctions (e.g. $x_1 + x_3 + \bar{x}_5$) requires exponentially many examples for information theoretic reasons (i.e. independent of computation) if only positive examples are available [41,75,26].

4.3 Irrelevant Attributes

We view learning as most interesting when it is allowed to be hierarchical. When learning a new concept we assume that it has a short description involving few variables, but these variables can be either primitives of the input devices or the outputs of much higher level functions previously programmed or learned. In human learning the number of concepts recognized at any time has been estimated as upwards of 10^5. Hence we have to aim at situations in which the number of variables n is of this order, but most of them are irrelevant to any one new concept. Having the sample complexity grow linearly with n is unsatisfactory.

We could hypothesize that humans have, in addition to induction capabilities, a focusing mechanism that on semantic grounds identifies which ten, say, of the 10^5 variables are really relevant. This, however, is exactly what we wish to avoid. We would like to absorb this "relevance identification" within the learning task, rather than leave it unexplained.

The first indication that this might be possible was a result of Haussler [32]. He showed that, among other things, learning conjunctions of length k over n variables could be done from only $O(k \log n)$ examples. The reduction of the dependence on n from linear to logarithmic is the significant point here. Littlestone [55] subsequently showed that the same effect could be achieved by a very elegant class of algorithms that resembled the classical perceptron algorithm but used a multiplicative update rule.

Very recently in a further surprising development Blum [14] described a context in which the learning of short hypotheses could be made independent of the total number of variables. Here each example is described by a set of variables that indicate the ones that are positive in the example. The complexity of learning certain Boolean formulae such as conjunctions can be bounded by an expression in terms of the length of description of the examples and of the hypothesis, even in an infinite attribute space.

4.4 Heuristics

The assumption in the basic model that the examples are totally consistent with a rule from a known class is one which one would like to relax. Error models offer one direction of relaxation. A second approach is to have the hypotheses learned still belong to a known class, but now regard them as heuristics in the sense that they account only for a certain percentage of the examples, say 80%. It may be that there is a simple rule of thumb that explains such a sizable percentage of examples, but that a much more complex hypothesis would be required to explain a larger fraction. It turns out that learning heuristics, even when they are simple conjunctions, is more difficult than in the basic model [64,78].

4.5 Learning Functions

Learning Boolean predicates is a special case of the problem of learning more general functions. Haussler [33] has given an interesting formulation of this in the spirit of the pac model. An important instance of function learning is that of learning distributions. Instead of having a hypothesis that predicts whether an example is a member of the concept, it now outputs a probability. In spite of the greater generality of this formulation, Kearns and Schapire [45] have shown that positive results can be obtained in this framework also.

4.6 Reliable and Useful Learning

In some contexts one may wish for hypotheses that are reliable in the sense that they never misclassify. In a probabilistic setting this is too much to expect unless one allows the hypothesis to output "don't know" in some cases. Rivest and Sloan [68] have shown that such a model is viable and plays a significant role in hierarchical learning. Reliable learning becomes useful, in their sense, if the probability of a "don't know" is suitably small. Reliable and useful learning is a much more demanding model than the basic one and has been applied only in very restricted cases [47].

4.7 Limiting the Computational Model

In all of the above we required that computations be performed in polynomial time on a general purpose model of computation such as a Turing machine. Since biological nervous systems have particular characteristics it is natural to ask how these results change if we restrict the models of computation appropriately. Such results have been obtained for certain models that are efficiently parallel [82,20], space bounded [24], or attempt to model neural systems directly [79].

4.8 Unsupervised Learning

Many learning situations involve no teacher labeling examples as positive or negative. The case when a totally passive world is observed by the learner is called unsupervised learning. A simple instance of unsupervised learning is that of detecting pairs of attributes that occur with high correlation [62]. More generally it is associated with clustering and other statistical techniques. A point of view put forward in [78,79] is that the most plausible way of overcoming the apparent limitations of both supervised and unsupervised learning separately is to combine them. For example, no effective algorithm is currently known for learning disjunctive normal form expressions in general. On the other hand one can imagine a system that learns special cases by the following two-tier strategy: It first learns conjunctions in some unsupervised sense, such as by detecting those pairs or n-tuples of variables that occur with high statistical correlation. In a separate stage it then learns a disjunction of these in supervised mode. It is possible that in human learning this kind of dynamic learning, where one alternates supervised and unsupervised phases, plays an important role.

5 Some Less Demanding Variants

5.1 Special Distributions

It is possible that in biological learning special properties of distributions are exploited. Unfortunately we have no indications as to what properties natural distributions have that make learning easier than for worst case distributions. As far as mathematical simplicity the obvious case to consider is when D^+ and D^- are uniform, and this case has received some attention.

For the distribution-free model an outstanding open problem is that of learning disjunctive normal form (DNF). Even when restricted to the uniform distribution DNF is not known to be learnable in polynomial time although it is learnable in time $n^{O(\log n)}$. Furthermore, the class of formulae with a constant number of alternations of conjunctions and disjunctions (so called constant depth circuits) is learnable in time exponential in $(\log n)^d$ where the d depends on the depth [53].

Some restrictions of DNF that are NP-hard to learn in the general model become learnable for the uniform distribution. These are μ-DNF, where each variable occurs once [41], and k-term DNF, where the disjunction is over k conjunctions [48,29,61].

Baum has considered uniformly distributed points on a sphere in the context of geometric concepts. He has shown that for learning half spaces better polynomial bounds can be obtained than in the general case [6]. On the other hand for learning the intersection of two half-spaces by the k-nearest neighbor algorithm exponential time is required [8].

The notion of learnability for fixed distributions has been analyzed by Benedek and Itai [12] and Natarajan [60].

Finally we note that other special distributions have been investigated also. Li and Vitanyi [51] consider one that is in some sense the hardest. Baum [7] considers distributions in Euclidean n-space that are symmetric about the origin, and shows that the intersection of two half spaces is learnable for these.

5.2 Ignoring Computation

As mentioned earlier if we ignore the computational aspect then we are back to purely statistical or information theoretic questions, which to within polynomial factors are trivial for discrete domains [17]. For infinite domains many issues come up which are more fully considered in [81,18,10,54,11]. The major tool here is the Vapnik-Chervonenkis dimension, which is a discrete quantity that characterizes the number of examples required for learning. The VC-dimension has been worked out for several concept classes. It is $n+1$, for example, for half-spaces in n dimensions. Furthermore for learning to within confidence δ and error ε fairly tight expressions are known on the number of examples needed [18,23]. One application given by Baum and Haussler [9] is to neural nets, where this kind of analysis has given guidance as to the number of examples needed for a generalization to be reliable.

6 Learning by Asking Questions

So far we have only considered passive learners. One would expect that a more aggressive learner who can ask questions would be a more successful one. This turns out to be the case. The basic model can be adapted easily to this more general case. For each kind of question we allow the learner to ask we hypothesize an oracle that is able to answer it. One such oracle is MEMBER. A call to this oracle with example x when the unknown concept is c would return "yes" or "no" depending on whether $x \in c$. Another oracle called EQUIVALENCE takes as input a hypothesis h and recognizes whether $h \equiv c$. If there is equivalence it outputs "yes". Otherwise it produces a counterexample to the equivalence.

For any fixed set of such oracles one can define learnability exactly as before except that the learning algorithm can consult one of these oracles in any one step [77]. If oracles are available one can also consider completely deterministic learning models where random draws from examples are dispensed with altogether. One such model is the "minimal adequate teacher" [2] which consists of the combination of MEMBER and EQUIVALENCE oracles. We note that the latter can be replaced by a probabilistic source of examples as in the pac model, since an equivalence $h \equiv c$ can be tested to a high degree of confidence by calling for enough random examples of c and checking for consistency with h. The deterministic model, however, often makes analysis more manageable in specific cases.

Several classes are now known to be learnable with such a minimal adequate teacher. These include deterministic finite automata [2], read-once Boolean formulae [4], and one-counter automata [13]. A number of related results are given in [3,30,69,70,72,27]. The issue of oracles is discussed more systematically in [3]. Allowing oracles appears to enlarge the range of positive results that can be obtained. The question of what constitutes a reasonable oracle, however, is unresolved. Clearly one can devise oracles that ask explicitly about the hypothesis, such as the identity of the ith line in the program defining it, that trivialize the learning problem. On the other hand membership oracles seem very plausible in relation to human learning.

7 Limits to What Can Be Learned

There are both information-theoretic and computational limitations to learning. Examples of the former already mentioned are the exponential lower bound on learning conjunctions from negative examples alone, and the lower bounds on sample complexity derived in terms of the Vapnik-Chervonenkis dimension.

Current knowledge suggests that the computational limitations are much more severe. Without it the class of all Boolean circuits (or any equivalent representation of discrete programs) is learnable. Once we insist on polynomial time computability only restricted subclasses are known to be learnable.

7.1 Representation-dependent Limits

Suppose we have an algorithm for learning C by the class H of representations. If we enlarge C then the problem will typically get more difficult. Enlarging H, on the other hand, and keeping C unchanged will typically make learning, if anything, easier since no more has to be learned but we have more ways of representing the hypotheses. Thus if H is learnable by H, then replacing H by a larger class H' could, in principle, make learning either harder or easier. In this sense learnable classes are not monotonic.

Another way of describing this phenomenon is the following. If C is not learnable by H, then this may be due to two reasons, either C is too large or H is too restricted. It turns out that existing techniques for proving NP-completeness impediments to learning are all of the second kind. Among the simplest classes C that are known to be hard to learn in this sense are 2-term DNF (i.e. disjunctions of two conjunctions) and Boolean threshold functions (i.e. half spaces of the form $\sum a_i x_i > b$ where each $a_i \in \{0,1\}$). For these classes learning C by C is NP-hard. In both cases, however, by enlarging C as functions we can obtain learnable classes. In the first case 2-CNF suffices, and in the second unrestricted half spaces ([64]). A further example of an NP-complete learning problem is the intersections of two half spaces [57]. This remains NP-complete even in the case of $\{0,1\}$ coefficients corresponding to certain three-node neural nets [16]. NP-hardness results are also known for learning finite automata [50,66,63] and other classes of neural nets [38,52].

7.2 Representation-independent Limits

As mentioned above there is a second reason for a class C not being learnable, in this case by any representation, and that is that C is too large. For reasons not well understood the only techniques known for establishing a negative statement of this nature are cryptographic. The known results are all of the form that if a certain cryptographic function is hard to compute then C is not learnable by any H. For such proofs the most natural choice of H is Boolean circuits since they are universal, and can be evaluated fast given their descriptions and a candidate input.

The first such result was implicit in the random function construction of Goldreich, Goldwasser and Micali [28]. It says that assuming one-way functions exist, the class of all Boolean circuits is not learnable even for the uniform distribution and even with access to a membership oracle. Various consequences can be deduced from this by means of reduction [65,83]

Since positive learning results are difficult to find even for much more restricted models it was natural to seek negative results closer to the known learnable classes. In [46] it was shown that deterministic finite automata, unrestricted Boolean formulae (i.e. tree structured circuits) and networks of threshold elements (neural nets) of a certain constant depth are each as hard to learn as it is to compute certain number-theoretic functions, such as factoring Blum integers (i.e. the products of two primes both equal to 3 mod 4) or inverting the RSA encryption function.

8 Models for Algorithm Discovery

Having precise models of learning seems to aid the discovery of learning algorithms. It focuses the mind on what has to be achieved. One significant finding has been that different models encourage different lines of thought and hence the availability of a variety of models is fruitful. Many of the algorithms discovered recently were developed for models that are either superficially or truly restrictions of the basic pac model.

One such model is that of learning from positive examples alone. This constraint suggests its own style of learning. Another model is the deterministic one using oracles discussed in section 6. Although the results for these translate to the pac model with oracles the deterministic formulation often seems the right one. A third promising candidate is the weak learning model. In seeking algorithms for classes not known to be learnable this offers a tempting approach which has not yet been widely exploited. We shall conclude by mentioning two further models both of which have proved very powerful.

The first is Occam learning [17]. After seeing random examples the learner seeks to find a hypothesis that is consistent with them and somewhat shorter to describe than the number of examples seen. This model implies learnability [17] and is essentially implied by it [19,73]. It expresses the idea that it is good to have a short hypothesis, but avoids the trap of insisting on the shortest one, which usually gives rise to NP-completeness even in the simplest cases. Occam learning can be generalized to arbitrary domains by relacing the bound on hypothesis size by a bound on the VC dimension [18].

There are many examples of algorithms that use the Occam model. These include algorithms for decision lists [67], restricted decision trees [22], semi-linear sets [1] and pattern languages [44].

The second model is that of worst-case mistake bounds [55]. Here after each example the algorithm makes a classification. It is required that for any sequence of examples there be only a fixed polynomial number of mistakes made. It can be shown that learnability in this sense implies pac learnability [3,41,56]. Recently Blum [15] showed that the converse is false if one-way functions exist.

There are a number of algorithms that are easiest to analyze for this model. The classical perceptron algorithm of Rosenblatt [71,58] has this form, except that in the general case the mistake bound is exponential. Littlestone's algorithms that perform well in the presence of irrelevant attributes [55], as well as Blum's more recent ones [14] are intimately tied to this model, as are a number of other algorithms including one for integer lattices [37].

References

[1] N. Abe. Polynomial learnability of semilinear sets. In *COLT*, pages 25–40 (1989).

[2] D. Angluin. Learning regular sets from queries and counter examples. *Information and Computation*, 75:87–106 (1987).

[3] D. Angluin. Queries and concept learning. *Machine Learning*, 2:319–342 (1987).

[4] D. Angluin, L. Hellerstein, and M. Karpinski. Learning read-once formulas with queries. Technical Report Rept. No. UCB/CSD 89/528, Computer Science Division and University of California and Berkeley (1989).

[5] D. Angluin and P. Laird. Learning from noisy examples. *Machine Learning*, 2:343–370 (1987).

[6] E. Baum. The perceptron algorithm is fast for non-malicious distributions. *Neural Computation*, 2:249–261 (1990).

The following abbreviations are used in the references:

COLT: Proceedings of Workshop on Computational Learning Theory, Morgan Kaufmann, San Mateo, CA

FOCS: Proceedings of the IEEE Symposium on Foundations of Computer Science, IEEE Computer Society Press, Washington, D.C.

STOC: Proceedings of the ACM Symposium on Theory of Computing, The Association for Computing Machinery, New York, NY

[7] E. Baum. A polynomial time algorithm that learns two hidden unit nets. In *COLT* (1990).

[8] E. Baum. When are k-nearest neighbor and back propagation accurate for feasible sized sets of examples? *Lecture Notes in Computer Science*, 412:2–25 (1990).

[9] E. Baum and D. Haussler. What size net gives valid generalization. *Neural Computation* 1(1):151–160 (1989).

[10] S. Ben-David, G. Benedek, and Y. Mansour. A parametrization scheme for classifying models of learnability. In *COLT*, pages 285–302 (1989).

[11] G. Benedek and A. Itai. Nonuniform learnability. Technical Report TR 474, Computer Science Department, Technion, Haifa, Israel (1987).

[12] G. M. Benedek and A. Itai. Learnability by fixed distributions. In *COLT*, pages 80–90 (1988).

[13] P. Berman and R. Roos. Learning one-counter languages in polynomial time. In *FOCS*, pages 61–67 (1987).

[14] A. Blum. Learning boolean functions in an infinite attribute space. In *STOC* (1990).

[15] A. Blum. Separating pac and mistake-bound learning models on the boolean domain. To appear, FOCS (1990).

[16] A. Blum and R. Rivest. Training a 3-node neural network is NP-complete. In *COLT*, pages 9–18 (1988).

[17] A. Blumer, A. Ehrenfeucht, D. Haussler, and M. Warmuth. Occam's razor. *Information Proc. Letters*, 25:377–380 (1987).

[18] A. Blumer, A. Ehrenfeucht, D. Haussler, and M. Warmuth. Learnability and the Vapnik-Chervonenkis dimension. *J. ACM*, 36(2):929–965 (1989).

[19] R. Board and L. Pitt. On the necessity of Occam algorithms. In *STOC* (1990).

[20] S. Boucheron and J. Sallantin. newblock Some remarks about space-complexity of learning, and circuit complexity of recognizing. In *COLT*, pages 125–138 (1988).

[21] T. Dietterich. Machine learning. *Ann. Rev. of Comp. Sci.*, 4 (1990).

[22] A. Ehrenfeucht and D. Haussler. Learning decision trees from random examples. *Inf. and Computation*, pages 231–247 (1989).

[23] A. Ehrenfeucht, D. Haussler, M. Kearns, and L. Valiant. A general lower bound on the number of examples needed for learning. *Inf. and Computation*, pages 247–261 (1989).

[24] S. Floyd. Space-bounded learning and the Vapnik-Chervonenkis dimension. *COLT*, pages 349–364 (1989).

[25] Y. Freund. Boosting a weak learning algorithm by majority. *COLT* (1990).

[26] M. Geréb-Graus. *Lower Bounds on Parallel, Distributed and Automata Computations*. PhD thesis, Harvard University (1989).

[27] S. Goldman, R. Rivest, and R. Schapire. Learning binary relations and total orders. In *FOCS*, pages 46–53 (1989).

[28] O. Goldreich, S. Goldwasser, and S. Micali. How to construct random functions. *J. ACM*, 33(4):792–807 (1986).

[29] Q. Gu and A. Maruoka. Learning monotone boolean functions by uniform distributed examples. Manuscript (1988).

[30] T. Hancock. Identifying μ-formula decision trees with queries. In *COLT* (1990).

[31] D. Haussler. Bias, version spaces and Valiant's learning framework. In *Proc. 4th Intl. Workshop on Machine Learning*, pages 324–336. Morgan Kaufmann (1987).

[32] D. Haussler. Quantifying inductive bias: AI learning algorithms and Valiant's learning framework. *Artificial Intelligence*, 36(2):177–222 (1988).

[33] D. Haussler. Learning conjunctive concepts in structural domains. *Machine Learning*, 4 (1990).

[34] D. Haussler, M. Kearns, N. Littlestone, and M. Warmuth. Equivalence of models of polynomial learnability. In *COLT*, pages 42–55 (1988).

[35] D. Haussler, N. Littlestone, and M. Warmuth. Predicting 0, 1-functions on randomly drawn points. In *COLT*, pages 280–296 (1988).

[36] D. Helmhold, R. Sloan, and M. Warmuth. Learning nested differences of intersection-closed concept classes. In *COLT*, pages 41–56 (1989).

[37] D. Helmhold, R. Sloan, and M. Warmuth. Learning integer lattices. In *COLT* (1990).

[38] J. Judd. Learning in neural nets. In *COLT*, pages 2–8 (1988).

[39] M. Kearns. *The Computational Complexity of Machine Learning*. MIT Press (1990).

[40] M. Kearns and M. Li. Learning in the presence of malicious errors. In *STOC*, pages 267–279 (1988).

[41] M. Kearns, M. Li, L. Pitt, and L. Valiant. On the learnability of Boolean formulae. In *STOC*, pages 285–295 (1987).

[42] M. Kearns, M. Li, L. Pitt, and L. Valiant. Recent results on Boolean concept learning. In *Proc. 4th Int. Workshop on Machine Learning*, pages 337–352, Los Altos, CA (1987). Morgan Kaufmann.

[43] M. Kearns, M. Li, and L. Valiant. Learning boolean formulae. To appear, JACM (1989).

[44] M. Kearns and L. Pitt. A polynomial-time algorithm for learning k-variable pattern languages from examples. In *COLT*, pages 57–71 (1989).

[45] M. Kearns and R. Schapire. Efficient distribution-free learning of probabilistic concepts. In *COLT* (1990).

[46] M. Kearns and L. Valiant. Cryptographic limitations on learning boolean formulae and finite automata. In *STOC*, pages 433–444 (1989).

[47] J. Kivinen. Reliable and useful learning. In *COLT*, pages 365–380 (1989).

[48] L. Kucera, A. Marchetti-Spaccamela, and M. Protasi. On the learnability of dnf formulae. In *ICALP*, pages 347–361 (1988).

[49] P. Laird. A survey of computational learning theory. Technical Report RIA-89-01-07-0, NASA, Ames Research Center (1989).

[50] M. Li and U. Vazirani. On the learnability of finite automata. In *COLT*, pages 359–370 (1988).

[51] M. Li and P. Vitanyi. A theory of learning simple concepts under simple distributions and average case complexity for the universal distribution. In *FOCS*, pages 34–39 (1989).

[52] J.-H. Lin and S. Vitter. Complexity issues in learning by neural nets. In *COLT*, pages 118–133 (1989).

[53] N. Linial, Y. Mansour, and N. Nisan. Constant depth circuits, Fourier transforms and learnability. In *FOCS*, pages 574–579 (1989).

[54] N. Linial, Y. Mansour, and R. Rivest. Results on learnability and the Vapnik-Chervonenkis dimension. In *COLT*, pages 56–68 (1988).

[55] N. Littlestone. Learning quickly when irrelevant attributes abound: a new linear threshold algorithm. *Machine Learning*, 2(4):245–318 (1988).

[56] N. Littlestone. From on-line to batch learning. In *COLT*, pages 269–284 (1989).

[57] N. Megiddo. On the complexity of polyhedral separability. Technical Report RJ 5252, IBM Almaden Research Center (1986).

[58] M. Minsky and S. Papert. Perceptrons: an introduction to computational geometry. MIT Press (1988).

[59] B. Natarajan. On learning boolean functions. In *STOC*, pages 296–304 (1987).

[60] B. Natarajan. Probably approximate learning over classes of distributions. Manuscript (1990).

[61] T. Ohguro and A. Maruoka. A learning algorithm for monotone k-term dnf. In *Fujitsu IIAS-SIS Workshop on Computational Learning Theory* (1989).

[62] R. Paturi, S. Rajasekaran, and J. Reif. The light bulb problem. In *COLT*, pages 261–268 (1989).

[63] L. Pitt. Inductive inference, dfas and computational complexity. In K. Jantke, editor, *Analogical and Indictive Inference. Lecture Notes in Computer Science, volume 397*, pages 18–44. Springer-Verlag (1989).

[64] L. Pitt and L. Valiant. Computational limitations on learning from examples. *J. ACM*, 35(4):965–984 (1988).

[65] L. Pitt and M. Warmuth. Reductions among prediction problems: on the difficulty of predicting automata. In *Proc. 3rd IEEE Conf. on Structure in Complexity Theory*, pages 60–69 (1988).

[66] L. Pitt and M. Warmuth. The minimal consistent dfa problem cannot be approximated within any polynomial. In *STOC*, pages 421–432 (1989).

[67] R. Rivest. Learning decision lists. *Machine Learning*, 2(3):229–246 (1987).

[68] R. Rivest and R. Sloan. Learning complicated concepts reliably and usefully. In *COLT*, pages 69–79 (1988).

[69] R. L. Rivest and R. Schapire. Diversity-based inference of finite automata. In *FOCS*, pages 78–88 (1987).

[70] R. L. Rivest and R. Schapire. Inference of finite automata using homing sequences. In *STOC*, pages 411–420 (1989).

[71] F. Rosenblatt. *Principles of Neurodynamics: Perceptrons and the Theory of Brain Mechanisms*. Spartan Books, Washington, D.C. (1961).

[72] Y. Sakakibara. Learning context-free grammars from structural data in polynomial time. In *COLT*, pages 330–344 (1988).

[73] R. Schapire. On the strength of weak learnability. In *FOCS*, pages 28–33 (1989).

[74] G. Shackelford and D. Volper. Learning k-dnf with noise in the attributes. In *COLT*, pages 97–105 (1988).

[75] H. Shvaytser. A necessary condition for learning from positive examples. *Machine Learning*, 5:101–113 (1990).

[76] R. Sloan. Types of noise for concept learning. In *COLT*, pages 91–96 (1988).

[77] L. Valiant. A theory of the learnable. *Comm. ACM*, 27(11):1134–1142 (1984).

[78] L. Valiant. Learning disjunctions of conjunctions. In *Proc. 9th Int. Joint Conf. on Artificial Intelligence*, pages 560–566, Los Altos, CA (1985). Morgan Kaufmann.

[79] L. Valiant. Functionality in neural nets. In *Proc. Amer. Assoc. for Artificial Intelligence*, pages 629–634, San Mateo, CA (1988). Morgan Kaufmann.

[80] V. Vapnik. *Estimation of Dependencies Based on Empirical Data*. Springer-Verlag (1982).

[81] V. Vapnik and A. Y. Chervonenkis. On the uniform convergence of relative frequencies of events to their probabilities. *Theor. Probability and Appl.*, 16(2):264–280 (1971).

[82] J. Vitter and J.-H. Lin. Learning in parallel. In *COLT*, pages 106–124 (1988).

[83] M. Warmuth. Toward representation independence in pac learning. In K. Jantke, editor, *Analogical and Inductive Inference, vol 397, Lecture Notes in Computer Science*, pages 78–103. Springer-Verlag (1989).

Chapter 4
Mappings Between High-Dimensional Representations of Acoustic and Visual Speech Signals

Terrence J. Sejnowski*   Ben P. Yuhas[†]

1 Introduction

The continued dramatic improvements in the speed and accessibility of general purpose digital computers has made it possible to model the brain at many different levels of investigation, from biophysical mechanisms to neural systems (Figure 1). However, the disparity between the computational power of even the fastest digital computers and that of the brain limits present simulations to a tiny fraction of the entire brain (Sejnowski [13]), or to creatures with only a few neurons (Selverston [15]). It is possible, for example, to model the information flow inside the dendrites and axons of single neurons, taking into account realistic anatomical and physiological details (Koch & Segev [8]). The study of networks of model neurons is just beginning. Some progress has been made by simplifying the details of single neurons in the network; such "neural network" models are primarily concerned with how the architecture of a network affects its capacity to perform a task and how the size of the network scales with the complexity of the task. In addition, systems-level architectural constraints from the brain at the level of columns of neurons, maps of neurons, and processing hierarchies can also be explored by modeling studies (Sejnowski & Churchland [14]).

One major difference between digital computers and brains is in the organization of memory. In conventional digital computers, memory is separated from the central processing unit and there is a communications bottleneck between them. Memory is expensive so that there is a premium on exploring algorithms that minimize the need for information storage. In contrast, the brain has a much greater capacity for storing information. The nervous system of man has approximately 10^{12} neurons and 10^{16} synapses, or connections between pairs of neurons. If every synapse could store only 1 bit

---

*The Salk Institute and University of California, San Diego, La Jolla, CA.
[†]Bell Communications Research, Morristown, New Jersey.

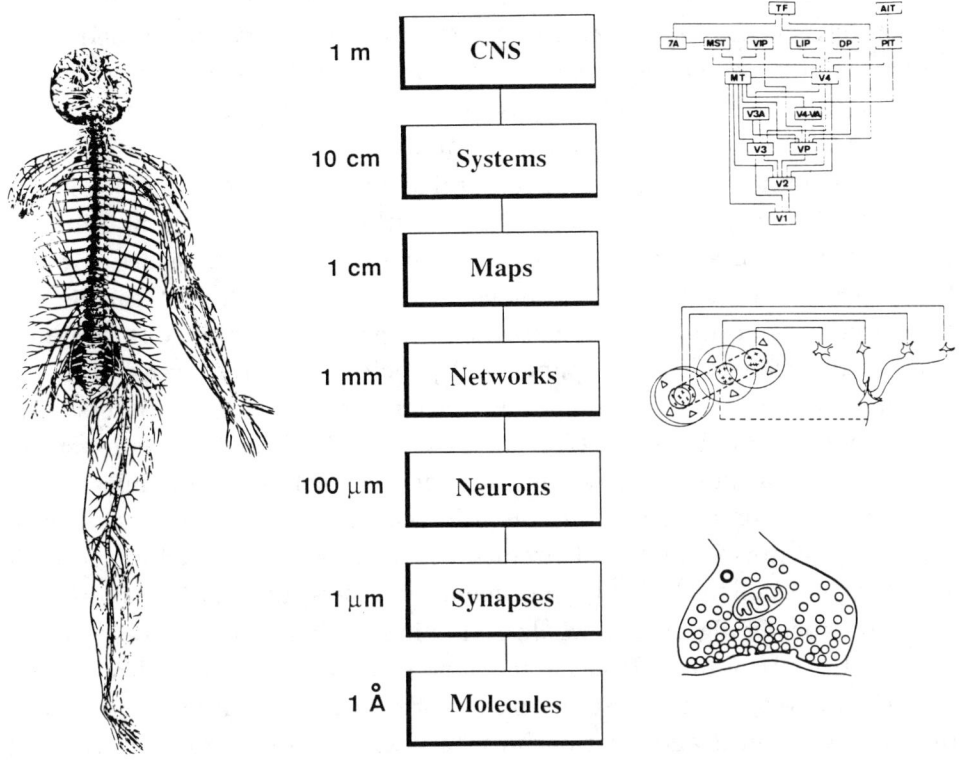

Figure 1:
Levels of investigation in the nervous system. The spatial scale on the left of the figure is related to the anatomical structures represented by each box. The schematic diagrams on the right illustrate the hierarchy of visual processing centers (top), the integration of input from the retina to form oriented receptive fields in the visual cortex (center), and the structure of a chemical synapse (bottom).

of information, the total capacity of the brain would still be over 10 million megabytes. Furthermore, all of this information is available on line, since the nonlinear processing elements in neurons are intertwined with the storage elements. These numbers probably underestimate the complexity of the brain because they do not take into account the continuous variables that are dynamically active during the processing within neurons and synapses. For example, there are biochemical mechanisms within synapses that modulate the strengths of synapses on a short time scale, over milliseconds, and others that produce changes that can last for years. It is these biochemical mechanisms that allow us to remember what happened a few minutes ago and to recall events in our childhood (Squire [16]).

Another major difference between brains and digital computers is in the way that information is manipulated. Algorithms for digital computers exploit the ability of a central processing unit to perform sequences of operations with great accuracy. In contrast, the logical depth that can be implemented by neural systems is not nearly as great—our ability to compute recursive functions without a paper and pencil is relatively weak. Finally, the brain should really be compared to a large number of computers, perhaps several hundred, rather than a single one. Each of these subsystems is dedicated to a different function, but they are able to communicate and cooperate to accomplish difficult tasks in real time. Some of these special purpose computers have neural circuits that can be reorganized by learning to solve new problems. This type of memory is programmed by experience.

What types of algorithms would run efficiently on architectures that resembled those of brains? Because memory is abundant, it would no longer be necessary to form the most compact representation for a problem. Thus, objects in the world and relationships between them could be represented in high-dimensional spaces, and the entire representation could be permanently stored. Even the brain, however, does not have enough memory capacity to handle the complexity of the world if the only representations available were in the space of the stimuli and all possible relationships had to be explicitly stored. For example, the visual representations of objects at the level of pixel intensities is not a good one for expressing categorical relationships. Consequently, visual processing, which comprises nearly half of cerebral cortex, extensively modifies the representation of an object to make it partially invariant to photometric variables and spatial transformations. Similarly, relationships must also be represented in an invariant way. These high-level representations are still very rich ones that contain much information about the physical properties of the stimulus, including properties from other modalities and even information about the use of the object (Damasio [3]). It is these high-level representations that are used by the brain to perform content-addressed retrieval, to make perceptual decisions, and to perform sensory-motor coordination, such as reaching out and grasping an object.

Representations in artificial intelligence are primarily symbolic. Even when thinking in terms of massively-parallel networks, there is a tendency to use discrete, low-dimensional representations, which have computational as well as conceptual advantages (Feldman [5], Valiant [18]). However, at least as a working hypothesis we would like to explore the possibility that cognitive tasks could be performed in the brain by mappings between high-dimensional spaces that constitute high-level representations of the sensory world and our possible interactions with it. Thus, the goal of our research is to understand a number of interlocking problems: What properties should high-dimensional distributed representations have to make them robust, efficient and flexible? Can mappings between these representations be performed that honor the computational structure of the tasks that must be accomplished? What can we learn from human performance that can help constrain possible network solutions?

In this paper we will explore these questions in the context of a specific problem in speech processing. The traditional approaches to speech recognition start with acoustic signals and end up with symbolic representations of distinctive features, phonemes, syllables, words, phrases and sentences. This approach ignores the speech information contained in other sensory modalities, such as the visual speech signals from the face of the speaker. Other sources of information relevant to speech include gestures, facial expressions, and even face color through stimulation of the autonomic nervous system. If the ultimate goal of a speech system is to extract semantic information from the speech stream, then these alternative sources of information could be important and perhaps make the interpretation of the acoustic signals much easier.

Petajan [11] has explored the visual speech signals for isolated digit recognition. In his system, the acoustic and visual speech information were independently reduced to symbol strings, and a set of rules was used to reconcile conflicting interpretations. The symbolic intermediates were needed to allow the necessary processing and integration to be performed in real time on the serial digital computers available. The massively-parallel architecture of artificial neural networks make it feasible to explore subsymbolic alternatives to Petajan's system. The use of high-dimensional representations allows information from several sources to be combined "softly," before being reduced to discrete symbols. In addition, learning algorithms provide a means of training networks to fuse these signals without explicit rules or restrictive a priori models. We will summarize recent results in visual speech recognition based on this new approach (Yuhas et al. [21]).

2 Neural Networks

The primary computational technique we used was mappings between high-dimensional vector spaces implemented with multilayer neural network models. The key features of these models are a large number of relatively simple nonlinear processing units and a high degree of connectivity between these units. A unit performs a nonlinear transformation on the sum of its inputs to produce a continuous output signal. When this output signal travels across a connection to another unit, the signal is attenuated or amplified by the weight associated with that connection. Computation is performed by the interaction of these units and signals. These models differ significantly from actual neural circuits found in the nervous systems. For example, the processing units used in this study simply add their weighted inputs and have a static sigmoidal nonlinear output function, while neurons in real nervous systems have more complex spatiotemporal nonlinearities and are capable of much more complex discriminations. Nevertheless, these networks provide a starting point for finding alternative approaches to difficult computational problems.

Feedforward network architectures were used in most of this study (Figure 2). The units in a feedforward network were arranged in layers, with connections only allowed between layers, and only in one direction. The units that receive inputs from outside the network are referred to as input units, and those that are observed from outside the network are output units. The remaining units are referred to as hidden, because they only exchange signals with other parts of the network. The units themselves use a nonlinear sigmoid squashing function to transform the sum of their inputs (Figure 2). The standard multilayered feedforward networks with arbitrary squashing functions are a class of universal approximators (White [19]). Moreover, any nonlinear mapping can be learned by a network if there are sufficient data to characterize the mapping and if the number of parameters in the network matches the information content of the data (White [20]).

A modified backpropagation algorithm was used to train feedforward networks (Rumelhart et al. [12]). The gradient was calculated in the standard manner, but instead of using steepest descent, a conjugate-gradient algorithm was used to update the weights. The number of adjustable weights in a neural network can often exceed the number of training patterns. In these cases, the networks have too many free parameters and are subject to the problem of overfitting or overlearning the training data. The effects of overlearning can be minimized by increasing the size of the training data set, by reducing the number of hidden units, by adding terms to the cost function that penalize unnecessary weights, or by stopping the training before the network has completely converged.

There is a natural statistical interpretation for the signals carried on the

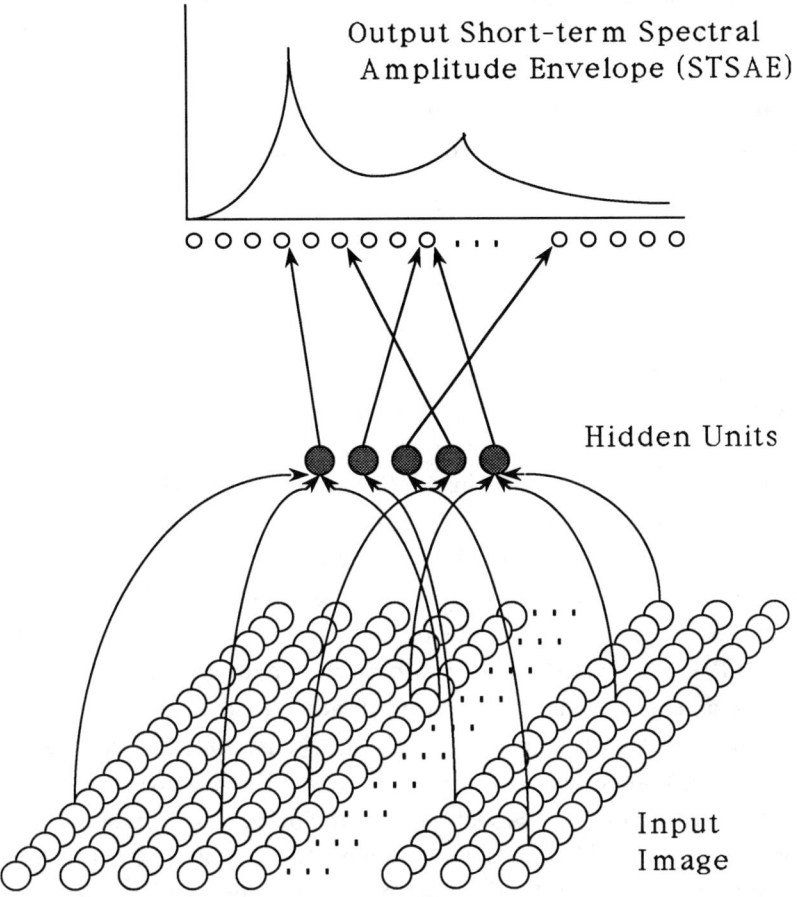

Figure 2:
Network architecture used for estimating the acoustic structure from visual speech signals. The feedforward network has 500 input units all connected to 5 hidden units, each in turn are fully connected to 32 output units. Each output unit represents the amplitude of the vocal tract transfer function at a particular frequency. The processing units in the network have a nonlinear input-output function given by: $f(x) = 1/(1 + exp(-x))$.

output units when the inputs are noisy. If the probability distribution of output units is Gaussian around a desired mean (for a mapping task), then the mean squared error used to train the network is the maximum likelihood cost function if the output units are linear (Bridle [2]; Rumelhart and Durbin, personal communication). A similar result holds for the output units if the probability distribution is binomial (for a binary categorization task) and the output units are sigmoidal. Then the correct maximum likelihood cost function is mutual information or information gain (Hinton & Sejnowski [6]).

3 The Speech Signals

The speech signals used were obtained from video recordings of a seated speaker facing a camera under well-lit conditions. The visual and acoustic signals were stored on a laser disc (Bernstein & Eberhardt [1]) where the individual frames and their corresponding speech segments were indexed. The NTSC video standard was used (30 frames/sec) and each frame had 33 milliseconds (ms) of speech associated with it. Phonemes usually are shortened or dropped altogether during fluent speech, so single video frames often span more than one phoneme. To avoid this problem, we selected speech samples such as stressed vowels in isolated word or consonant-vowel-consonant (CVC) type nonsense syllables that change relatively slowly. In these contexts, the vowels often were steady state over periods of 50 to 100 ms. For a given phoneme, a preliminary list of candidate words was identified from a transcription of the laser disc. Each word was then played acoustically to confirm the suspected pronunciation. A representative frame for the vowel was then isolated by alternately dropping a frame and then listening until the surrounding consonants were removed. The number of frames that remained after this process depended upon the degree to which that particular vowel was stressed. Stressed vowels, for example, can last up to 132 ms or 4 frames, while an unstressed vowel in continuous speech will often not last the full 33 ms of a single frame. The acoustic signals of the remaining frames were digitized and visually examined to ensure that acoustic signal was approximately in steady state. From this set, a single frame was selected only if the periodic wave form appeared relatively stable, neither increasing nor decreasing in amplitude. This paper describes results obtained using data from a single male speaker. A data set was constructed of 108 images of 9 different vowels in 12 sets. The vowels were taken from words and CVCs. Because these words and syllables were spoken deliberately and in isolation, these vowels were isolated easily. Data from a female speaker were also studied.

Instead of searching for an optimal encoding of the input images, we chose a simple representation that seemed to contain the relevant information. A rectangular area-of-interest was automatically defined and centered about the mouth. The image was further reduced to produce an image that could be comfortably handled by our network simulations. Within the rectangle, the average value of each 4 x 4 pixel square was computed to produce a topographically accurate grey-scale image of 20 x 25 pixels. Rather than attempt to extract special features, this encoding represented a form that could be obtained easily through an array of analog photoreceptors. Two methods of processing these images of the speaker's mouth were explored. In the first approach, we treated the images categorically and attempted to make hard phonemic decisions directly from the images. Such linguistic identifications can be used to constrain the linguistic interpretation of a noise-degraded acoustic signal. In the second approach, we obtained acoustic information directly from the images by estimating the transfer function of the vocal tract. These independent estimates were then used to constrain the acoustic interpretation of the noise-degraded acoustic signal directly.

The acoustic speech signal emitted from the mouth can be modeled as the response of the vocal-tract filter to a switchable sound source. In a first-order vocal-tract model, the configuration of the articulators (e.g, the mouth opening, the lips, teeth, tongue, velum and glottis) defines the shape of the vocal tract filter, which then determines the filter's frequency response. The resonances of the vocal tract filter appear as peaks in the envelope of the short-term power spectrum of the acoustic signal and are called formants. While some of the articulatory features are often visible (e.g., the lips, teeth and sometimes the tongue), other components of the articulatory system, such as the glottis and velum, are not. Those articulators that are visible tend to modify the acoustic signal in ways that are more susceptible to acoustic distortion than those effects due to the hidden articulators. This complementary structure can be exploited to improve the perception of speech in noise.

4 Categorization

Neural networks were trained to identify the vowel directly from the image. The images were presented across 500 input units, and the output consisted of 9 output units, each representing one of the nine vowels in the data. An input image was correctly categorized when the activation value of the correct vowel unit was larger than all the other output units. The data set of 108 images was split into a test set and a training set of 54 images, each containing a balanced set of vowels. The number of hidden units were varied. A network was trained until the categorization of all 54 images in the training set was perfect. Overtraining was minimized by immediately terminating the training at this point, before the output units were driven to saturation. After the network was trained, it then was tested on the second set of 54 images from the same speaker.

Performance levels were averaged across eight networks having five hidden units, each initialized with different random weights. The networks were trained on 54 patterns. For half of the networks, the training and test sets were reversed. The eight networks trained on the male data obtained an average performance of 76% correct categorizations for the images in the test set. A nearest neighbor classifier was constructed using the training data as the set of stored templates and the results compared with the performance of the neural network model. The individual images from the test set were correlated with the stored templates, and the image was classified according to its closest match. The process was repeated again, but with the test and training sets reversed. The nearest neighbor classifier correctly classified the male data set with an average accuracy of 79%. The performance of the network also compared favorably with two human subjects tested and trained on the same data. After 5 training sessions, the two subjects obtained an average of 70% on the images in the test set, with performances in some follow-up sessions approaching 80%. The types of errors made by the human subjects in these experiments were similar to those made by the network as judged by comparing the confusion matrices.

5 Precategorical Fusion

Summerfield [17] concluded from psychoacoustic experiments that information from the visual and acoustic modalities must be integrated before phonetic or lexical categorization takes place. The implication was that the acoustic and visual signal streams shared a common representation at their conflux. We have used the vocal tract transfer function as a model for this common representation, and we have shown that networks can be designed for integrating visual and acoustic speech signals using this representation (Yuhas et al. [21]). An estimate of the vocal tract's acoustic characteristics was obtained directly from images of the speaker's mouth. This estimate then served as an independent source of acoustic information and was used to constrain the interpretation of the acoustic signal.

The acoustic speech signal is produced by a source signal that passes through the vocal tract and is emitted from the mouth. For voiced speech, the driving signal is a quasi-periodic pulse train convolved with the glottal wave form. This driving signal's contribution to the short-term acoustic spectrum is a series of harmonics reducing in amplitude by -12 dB per octave. This reduction is partially compensated by the radiation of the acoustical signal from the lips, which produces an effective gain of +6 dB per octave. The spectral envelope of the short-term spectrum that remains after these two effects are removed is the frequency response of the vocal tract filter. The transfer function of the vocal tract can be estimated by measuring the short-term spectral amplitude envelope (STSAE) of the acoustic signal.

There is not enough information in the visual speech signal to completely specify the vocal-tract transfer function. Many different acoustic signals can be produced by vocal tract configurations that correspond to the same visual signal. Thus, the visual signals can provide only a partial description of the vocal tract filter. Nonetheless, it may be possible to obtain a good estimate of the vocal tract transfer function if additional constraints are considered. A feedforward neural network was trained to estimate the STSAE of the acoustic signal directly from the visual signals around the mouth. The estimate of the STSAE was then combined with estimates from acoustic information to improve the signal-to-noise ratio prior to recognition. The same images of the male speaker used in the categorization experiments were used in these experiments. Each video frame had 33 ms of acoustic speech associated with it. The short-term power spectra of the corresponding acoustic data were calculated and the spectral envelopes were obtained using cepstral analysis. Each smoothed envelope was sampled at 32 frequencies to produce a vector of scalar values. These vectors were used to represent the vocal-tract transfer functions corresponding to the images.

Vowels are largely identified by their spectral shape, and in particular by the location of their spectral peaks, or formants. Nevertheless, evaluating the quality of these spectral estimates is significantly more difficult than judging the accuracy of a categorization because the perceptual processes involved in processing the spectral peaks is not a well-understood process. To assay our spectral estimates, a simple vowel recognition system was constructed using a simple feedforward network trained to recognize nine vowels from their STSAEs. The network was trained on 6 examples each of 9 different vowels until its performance was 100% on the training data. This network served as a perfect recognizer of the noise-free data and was used to assess the benefit of the visually-estimated spectra when combined with the noise-degraded acoustic spectra.

The vowel recognizer was presented with a STSAE through two channels. The path shown on the right in Figure 3 was for the information obtained from the acoustic signal, while the path on the left provided spectral estimates obtained independently from the corresponding visual speech signal. The first step was to test the performance of the recognizer when the acoustic spectral envelopes were degraded by noise. Zero-mean random vectors were normalized and added to the training STSAEs to produce signals with signal-to-noise ratios ranging from -12 dB to 24 dB. Noise corrupted vectors were produced at 3 dB intervals from -12 dB to 24 dB. At each noise level, 12 different vectors were produced for each of the STSAE in the set. At each level, the performances of the recognizer on the degraded signals were

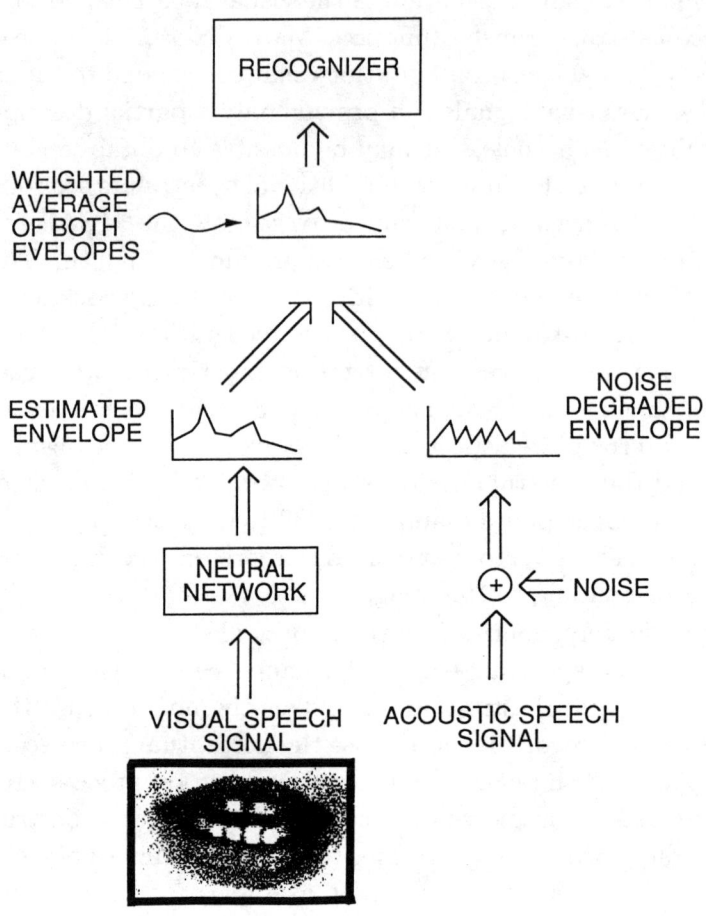

Figure 3:
System used to combine visual and acoustic speech information. A simple vowel recognizer was constructed to receive speech signals from the two modalities. Independent estimates of the vocal tract transfer function were produced and then combined with a weighted average before being passed to the recognizer. A neural network was trained to perform the mapping of the image into the estimated envelope of the acoustic spectra. Noise was introduced into the acoustic speech signal and the improvement due to the visual information was assessed.

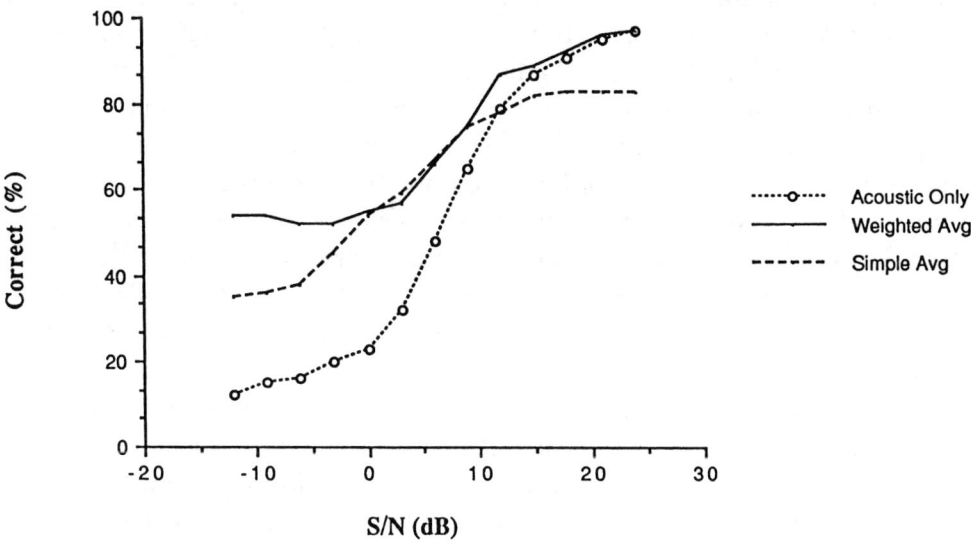

Figure 4:
Intelligibility of noise-degraded speech as a function of speech-to-noise ratio in dB. The lower curve shows the performance of the recognizer under varying signal-to-noise conditions using only the acoustic channel. The intermediate dashed curve shows the performance when the two independent estimates are equally weighted. The top curve shows the improved performance by using a weighting function based on the signal-to-noise. When the visual signal is used alone, the percent correct is 55% across all S/N levels.

averaged. The overall performance on the training data fell with decreased signal-to-noise ratios. At -12 dB, the recognizer operated at the chance level, which was 11% with nine vowels in the data set.

The next step was to compensate for the noise degradation by providing an independent estimate of the STSAE from the visual signal, as shown on the left side of Figure 3. The network on this pathway was trained to estimate the spectral envelopes corresponding to the input images. The data used to train this network were different from the data used to train the recognizer. The noise-degraded acoustic signal was then combined with the output from the network processing the images to provide a single estimate which is then passed on to the recognizer. The acoustic and visual signals were weighted according to their relative information content to compensate for the degraded performance at the signal-to-noise ratio extremes. The optimal value of the weighting was found empirically to vary approximately linearly with the signal-to-noise ratio in dB, from 1 at -12 dB signal-to-noise ratio to 0 at 24 dB. The performance is shown in Figure 4. Another method of fusing the two spectra was accomplished using a sigma-pi neural network (Rumelhart et al. [12]). These second-order networks took the estimated

STSAE, the noise-degraded acoustic STSAE and a measure of the signal-to-noise ratio as input, and tried to produce a noise-free STSAE as output. In contrast to the simple weighted sum used by first-order units, the units in these second-order networks determine the activation level by summing the weighted product or other units' output. The results from this method were mixed: while the squared-error between the estimated and actual spectra was significantly lower, their categorization was poorer. These results suggest that the vowel recognizer is doing something more complicated than simply making a comparison based upon a squared-error measure. It also raises questions as to the appropriateness of the mean squared-error measure used for training.

The quality of the estimates made by the networks were compared to a combination of two optimal linear-estimation techniques. The first step was to encode the images using a Hotelling or Karhunen-Loeve transform. The images were encoded as five-dimensional vectors defined by the largest principal components of the covariance matrix of the images in the training set. This is an optimal encoding of the images with respect to a least-squared-error (LSE) measure. The next step was to find a mapping from these encoded image vectors to their corresponding short-term spectral amplitude envelopes (STSAEs). The fit was found using a linear least-squares fit. The estimates obtained by this two stage process were significantly poorer in overall mean-squared error. The mean-squared error of the estimates made by the networks were 46% better on the training set and 12% better on the test set. This comparison shows that arbitrary encoding of the images may result in a loss of relevant information. In contrast, the network learning algorithm allows the network to produce its own encoding at the hidden layer based upon relevant features. The activation levels of the five hidden units served to encode the image as did the five-dimensional vectors obtained using principal components. The primary difference is that the encoding found by the network optimized the desired output, while the principal components optimized the LSE reconstruction of the images.

6 Dynamics and Speech

In the models described thus far, attention was restricted to static visual images, which were inherently ambiguous because they contain incomplete information about the speech articulators. Speech is a dynamic process and the articulators are physical structures that move. Their current positions are part of larger dynamic trajectories. These trajectories are constrained by the mechanics of the physical system and by the linguistic rules of the language. Dynamic dependencies could provide additional constraints that can serve to restrict the acoustic interpretation of the visual speech signal.

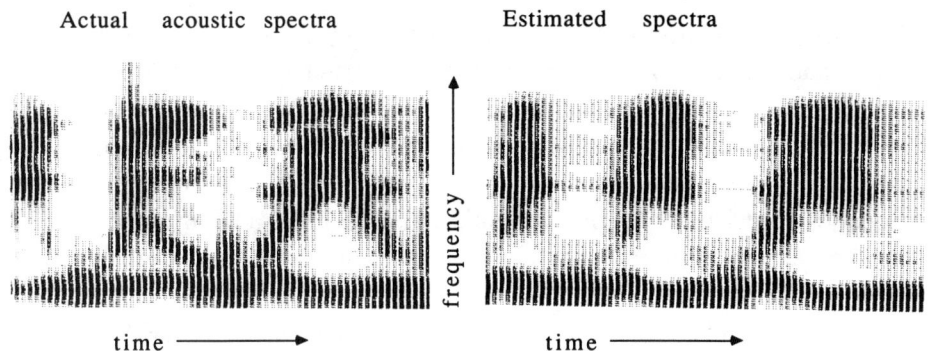

Figure 5:
Spectrograms created from the actual acoustic spectra are compared to visually-estimated spectra for the sentence: "We will weigh you". Individual spectral estimates were converted to a grey scale and then aligned by frequency as a function of time. Actual acoustic data from the test set are shown on the left and estimates produced by the feedback neural network model are shown on the right.

In this section, we outline an approach to introducing dynamic constraints in neural network models. One approach is to have projections from the output units to the input layer (Jordan [7]) or from hidden units to the input layer (Elman [4]).

When working with static images, it was possible to use a simple vowel recognizer to test the quality and utility of the acoustic spectra estimated from static images. The success of the vowel recognizer depended on the careful selection of vowels from isolated words or syllables. For continuous speech, however, it is difficult and often impossible to make these definitive identifications of short speech segments taken out of context, so alternative assessments are necessary. Networks with feedback were used to estimate the STSAE from images within a larger context. The performance of the network on continuous speech was evaluated on its ability to preserve the salient features of the spectral sequences, such as the resonances, or formants, of the estimated vocal tract filter. To see how well these formants were identified by the network, the sequences of spectra were arranged in a visual display similar to a spectrogram. The spectrogram shown in Figure 5 was created from spectra estimated from a sequence of images not in the training set. In this form, we can observe the changes of energy in the different frequency bands as a function of time. Clearly, much of the acoustic structure was being estimated in these sequences. The ultimate test will be to either resynthesize the acoustic speech signal from these estimated acoustic parameters, or to feed the fused spectra into a full-scale speech recognizer.

7 Discussion

Under noisy conditions, speech recognition using acoustic information alone degrades and performance can be aided by extracting information from the visual speech signals and combining it with residual acoustic information. Two representations for the speech information in the visual signal were studied. In the first case the visual signal was treated symbolically, while in the second it was used to provide subsymbolic information about the corresponding acoustic signal. These are two points on a continuum of speech descriptions. Other representations of the speech signals, such as descriptions of the articulators themselves, could also have been used. It would valuable to know what representations are used in the brain. A better understanding of the visual and acoustic sensory systems in humans and other animals will lead to better artificial sensors and their effective integration.

By combining the visual and acoustic sources of speech information, we have demonstrated that the visual signal can be used to improve the performance of automatic vowel recognition in the presence of noise. This approach did not require categorical preprocessing or explicit rules. The performances of these neural networks compared favorably with human performance and with other pattern-matching and estimation techniques. Our results were based on vowels spoken by single speakers, but this same approach can be extended to multiple speakers and to consonants. Improvements can also be made in the input representations. Synthetic cochleas that can process massive amounts of sensory data in real time already have been fabricated in analog VLSI (Mead [10]). The output of these chips is a highly distilled, parallel and distributed representation of the acoustic signal. These front-ends could improve the overall level of performance of acoustic speech recognition systems, but they would not change our conclusions concerning the need to compensate for noise – they only put off the inevitable.

The results from the specific examples studied in this paper can be generalized to many other problems that depend on the fusion of information from several cues or from several modalities (Lehky et al. [9]). The key idea is to represent the information in a distributed way and to rely on high-dimensional mappings from these cues into a common representation. Learning algorithms can be used to seamlessly combine the two information streams, and to continuously adapt in nonstationary environments. At present, we are only able to guess which representations are likely to be good ones, based in part on what we know about the representations in the brain. We need a deeper understanding of distributed representations that can guide us in these choices. It is also likely that more sophisticated neural architectures will be needed to deal with the fusion of information, especially when there are conflicting sources of information.

Nature has been an inspiration for many mathematical discoveries. Much of functional analysis grew out of attempts to understand the physical world. The biological world is also a source of inspiration but the complexity of biological systems often exceeds our abilities to develop simple, analyzable, mathematical models. This is especially true in the study of the brain, a biological system with a degree of complexity greater than that of any other known system. As we learn more about the brain, and as we explore the function of the brain with a wide variety of mathematical and computational models, we may begin to develop an understanding of the computational principles of the brain comparable to our mathematical understanding of the physical world.

References

[1] Bernstein, L. E., Eberhardt, S. P., *Johns Hopkins Lipreading Corpus I-II*, Johns Hopkins University, Baltimore, MD (1986).

[2] Bridle, J. S., Probabilistic interpretation of feedforward classification network outputs, with relationships to statistical pattern recognition. In F. Fogelman-Soulie (Ed.), *Neuro-Computing: Algorithms, Architectures and Applications*, Springer-Verlag, Berlin (1989).

[3] Damasio, A. R., Category-related recognition as a clue to the neural substrates of knowledge, *Trends in Neuroscience*, **13**, 95-98 (1990).

[4] Elman, J. L., Finding structure in time, *Cognitive Science*, **14**, 179-211 (1990).

[5] Feldman, J., Technical Report TR-189: Neural representation of conceptual knowledge, University of Rochester Department of Computer Science (1986).

[6] Hinton, G., Sejnowski, T., Learning and relearning in Boltzmann machines. In J. L. McClelland & D. E. Rumelhart (Eds.), *Parallel Distributed Processing: Explorations in the Microstructure of Cognition: Psychological and Biological Models*, **Vol. 1**, *Foundations* MIT Press, Cambridge, MA, 282-317 (1986).

[7] Jordan, M. I., Supervised learning and systems with excess degrees of freedom, COINS Technical Report 88-27, Computer and Information Science, University of Massachusetts at Amherst (1988).

[8] Koch, C., Segev, I., *Methods in Neuronal Modeling: From Synapse to Networks*, MIT Press, Cambridge, MA (1989).

[9] Lehky, S. R., Pouget, A., & Sejnowski, T. J., Neural models of binocular depth perception. In E. R. Kandel, T. J. Sejnowski, C. F. Stevens,

J. D. Watson (Eds.) *Cold Spring Harbor Symposia on Quantitative Biology: The Brain*, **55**, Cold Spring Harbor, New York, Cold Spring Harbor Press (1990).

[10] Mead, C., *Analog VSLI and neural systems*, Addison-Wesley, Reading, MA (1989).

[11] Petajan, E. D., An improved Automatic Lipreading System To Enhance Speech Recognition, AT&T Bell Laboratories Technical Report No. 11251-871012-111TM, Murray Hill, NJ (1987).

[12] Rumelhart, D. E., Hinton, G. E., & Williams, R. J., Learning internal representations by error propagation. In J. L. McClelland & D. E. Rumelhart (Eds.) *Parallel Distributed Processing: Explorations in the Microstructure of Cognition*, **Vol. 1**, *Foundations* MIT Press, Cambridge, MA (1986).

[13] Sejnowski, T. J., Computing with connections: Review of "The Connection Machine" by W. Daniel Hillis. *Journal of Mathematical Psychology*, **31**, 203-210 (1987).

[14] Sejnowski, T. J., Churchland, P. S., Brain and cognition. In M. I. Posner (Ed.), *Foundations of Cognitive Science*, MIT Press, Cambridge, MA (1989)

[15] Selverston, A. I., A consideration of invertebrate central pattern generators as computational data bases, *Neural Networks*, **1**, 109-117 (1988).

[16] Squire, L., *Memory and Brain*, Oxford University Press, Oxford (1987).

[17] Summerfield, Q., Some preliminaries to a comprehensive account of audio-visual speech perception. In B. D. a. R. Campbell (Ed.), *Hearing by Eye: The Psychology of Lip Reading*, Lawrence Erlbaum Assoc., Hillsdale, NJ (1987).

[18] Valiant, L., this book.

[19] White, H., Some asymptotic results for learning in single hidden layer feedforward networks, *Journal of the American Statistical Association*, **85** (1989).

[20] White, H., Learning in artificial neural networks: A statistical perspective, *Neural Computation*, **1**, 425-464 (1990).

[21] Yuhas, B. P., Goldstein, M. H., Jr., Sejnowski, T. J. & Jenkins, R. E., Neural network models of sensory integration for improved vowel recognition, *Proc. IEEE* (October, 1990).

Chapter 5
Colligation of Coupled Cortical Oscillators by the Collapse of the Distributions of Amplitude-Dependent Characteristic Frequencies*

Walter J. Freeman[†]

Abstract

Neural information in the cerebral cortex is contained in patterns of spatial amplitude modulation of spatially coherent oscillations of neural activity. These waves emerge from the cooperative activities of neural populations that are distributed over extended regions comprising tens to hundreds of millions of neurons. Each local group or neighborhood consists of excitatory and inhibitory neurons that oscillate together through their negative feedback interaction. An intrinsic design problem is that the characteristic frequency of each such local oscillator is amplitude-dependent. Thus the variation in amplitude that is required to express neural information by modulation of the common oscillation can have a dispersive effect on the global cortical population around its mean frequency, thereby weakening it. Efficient coupling is enabled by two neural mechanisms that collapse the distribution of the characteristic frequencies of the oscillators. The design features that underlie these mechanisms are (a) the cable properties of the dendrites, which are approximated by use of a 2nd order ordinary differential equation as the kernel of integration, and (b) an excitatory bias from a subsidiary population of interneurons at the input. These two properties are found also to be necessary though not sufficient for the genesis of chaotic oscillations by neuron populations. Justification is given to incorporate these two features into artificial neural networks for pattern recognition, and references are cited to reports that demonstrate their utility.

1 Introduction

The information that is brought to the cerebral cortex by the axons of sensory neurons is transformed so as to be expressed in the amplitudes of induced

---

*This work was supported by grant MH06686 from NIMH and by grant AF88-0268 from AFOSR.

[†]Department of Molecular and Cell Biology, University of California at Berkeley.

oscillatory activity by coupled local populations of neurons [19,34]. The assembly of the discrete bits of information corresponding to "features" takes place by the interactive coupling among groups of excitatory and inhibitory neurons that comprise "oscillators" [15]. Experimentally this is seen to occur at a common instantaneous frequency of oscillation across a distributed array of cortical oscillators. Yet cortical activity shows strong tendencies to broad spectra and aperiodic oscillations. We also know that local characteristic frequencies are strongly dependent on interneural feedback gains, which are in turn dependent on the local amplitudes of oscillation, owing to the static sigmoid nonlinearity in the neural population dynamics [7,15,16]. The question is: how is a common frequency of oscillation maintained among a spatially distributed population of oscillators at widely differing amplitudes of oscillation, when the frequency tends to vary with amplitude?

Here it is shown that two design features of the cortex comprising the olfactory bulb serve to converge a distribution of local characteristic frequencies toward a shared frequency, that co-varies over time and thereby facilitates the sharing of sensory input in the formation of a percept over a broad spectrum. These features underlie read-out of the percept from the cortex at a high signal:noise ratio [21].

One feature is the time delay from the cable properties of the dendrites. The other is an excitatory bias which is contributed by mutually excitatory neurons, that are co-excited by sensory input and that act in parallel with the input onto the cortical neurons. These features counteract the tendency for variations in the amplitude of oscillation to disperse the local characteristic frequencies. Such dispersion would work against the sharing of sensory information among the coupled oscillators. It would also interfere with the read-out by the parts of the brain that receive the cortical output. Those parts operate on whatever they receive by the experimentally observed process of on-line, real-time spatial integration. It is denoted the "brain laundry" [21], because only that part of the transmission at the common instantaneous frequency of the shared waveform survives the integration as signal, and the residue is removed as "noise" by smoothing.

2   Experimental Bases and Premises

Oscillations in the electrical activity of the cerebral cortex take differing forms of complexity, ranging from almost periodic through quasiperiodic to aperiodic (pseudorandom or chaotic). The Fourier transform applied to single time series yields power spectra that respectively have a single peak, multiple peaks, or a monotonic fall-off in power with increasing frequency that may approximate that of "1/f noise." Irrespective of the form of the activity the following five properties have been found to hold for activity recorded from many parts of the cerebrum.

2.1 Spatial Coherence

The temporal waveforms of activity that are recorded simultaneously from electrodes placed on the surface of contiguous areas of cortex are substantially alike although not identical. Quantitative assays of the amount of covariance by use of Fourier decomposition [28] of olfactory cortical recordings and principal components analysis of visual cortical traces [27] have given estimates that 65% of the total variance on the average is incorporated into the first or dominant component of the variance. The degree of commonality is highly variable from moment to moment, ranging from under 20% to in excess of 90% in different behavioral conditions as well as randomly within conditions.

We infer from the shared oscillations that the cortex is comprised of neurons forming local groups that can be treated as coupled oscillators, and from the variability that the degree of coupling by synaptic action is subject to rapid fluctuations over time. From experimental data and modeling [15, 21] we infer that the oscillations are a global property, which is emergent from the coupling of very large numbers of neurons that are spatially dispersed over distances of tens of millimeters and centimeters.

2.2 Interneuronal Negative Feedback

Each neuron in the cortex transmits its output to other neurons by sending pulses along its axon to synapses at its terminals. These trains of pulses have two very important properties. First, the average firing rates are low, for most neurons substantially below 10 pulses/second. Yet the cortical frequencies of greatest interest for their content of behavioral information are from 20 to 90 Hz. Second, the intervals between successive pulses are highly variable and indeed unpredictable from one to the next pulse, so that the distributions of intervals in histograms conform to a Poisson process with a dead time.

These experimental facts exclude the possibility that the group oscillations observed in cortex result from coupling of single neurons that act as individual oscillators, as has been suggested for the cerebellum [31]. On the contrary, they must emerge from the feedback interaction of local populations of excitatory and inhibitory neurons. It follows immediately that within each area of cortex there must exist two sub-populations for which the oscillations at the common frequencies have, on the average, a quarter cycle phase lag between them, corresponding to the state variables of the forward and feedback limbs of negative feedback loops [15]. In all cases where these sub-populations have been sought, they have been found [21,2].

2.3 Fixed Time and Space Constants

Network models for cortical dynamics require three types of numerical coefficients: those for time delays, spatial distances of action, and strengths of action or gains. Experimentally we have found that the base frequencies are dependent on the time constants of neurons, principally the passive membrane decay rates that are determined by the biophysical properties of neural membranes and by the lengths and conduction velocities of axons. The space constants are determined by the radii of the extents of axons and dendrites of neurons. Experimentally we have found that these properties are truly constant over time periods that are substantially longer than the requirements for most behavioral information management by neuron populations.

These findings indicate that the time and space constants can be fixed at common values throughout a network as the open loop rate constants, and variable coefficients are introduced only in those parameters representing the coupling coefficients or gains. The determinants of coupling fall into two classes: short term and long term. The long term coefficients denote those changes that take place at synapses with learning processes such as association, facilitation and habituation. The short term changes take place at the sites of formation of pulses that are called trigger zones. In local sub-populations of neurons the trigger zones introduce a static nonlinearity in neurodynamics that is commonly called the "sigmoid curve" or "squash function" (Figure 1). The slope of the sigmoid curve gives a nonlinear gain, which has the shape of a bell, and which shows that the gain is a function of the amplitude of activity in the neuron group [7,15,16,20]. With increasing magnitude of depolarizing activity from excitatory synapses and also of hyperpolarizing activity at inhibitory synapses, there is asymptotic approach to a limit on the response to the inputs.

2.4 Piecewise Linearization

Each population performs four serial operation with each pass of the information through its limb. The activity on incoming axons is converted at the dendritic synapses to dendritic current by an operation $G_d(p)$ that converts afferent pulse density (p) to dendritic current density (v). The dendrites perform linear space-time integration $f_d(x, y, t)$. The resultant is converted to a pulse density function at the trigger zones of the neurons in the population in accordance with the sigmoid function $G_a(v)$. The output pulse density is transmitted, amplified and diverged by the axonal branches, $f_a(x, y, t)$.

The modeling of this serial processing, $G_d f_d G_a f_a$, is simplified in three ways. The distances and time delays in local networks are usually sufficiently small that the dynamics can be modeled with lumped elements, so the spatial dimensions are omitted. The nonlinear operation G_d at synapses is held

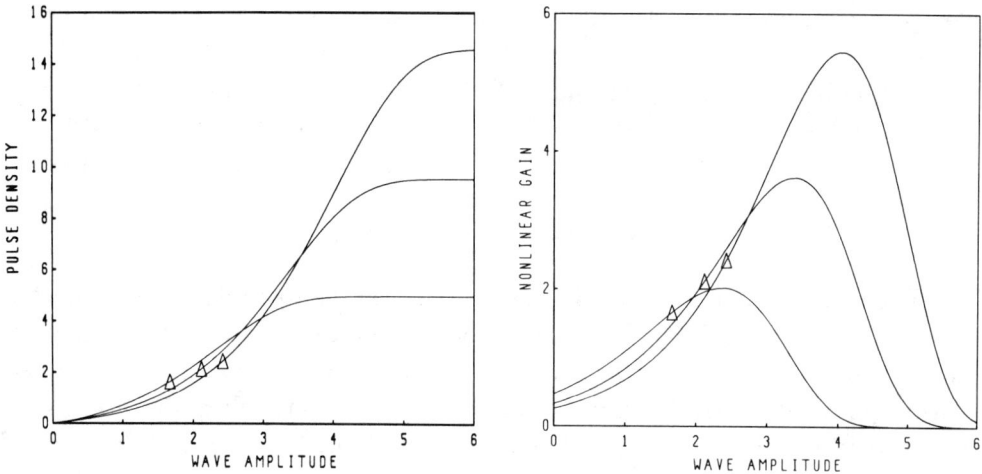

Figure 1:
These sigmoid curves have been derived by modification of the Hodgkin-Huxley system and have been fitted to experimental data that were derived from recordings of unit activity and local field potentials in the olfactory system of the cat. A single parameter Q_m serves to adapt the curve to different animals and behavioral states of arousal, where Q is normalized pulse rate and v is wave amplitude (left), Q_m is the maximal population pulse rate; and μ_o is defined by Q_m [16]:

$$Q = Q_m\{1 - \exp[-(e^v - 1)/Q_m]\}, \qquad v \geq -\mu_o, \qquad Q = -1, \qquad v < -\mu_o.$$

The lowest curve fits data taken under anesthesia. The middle curve corresponds to moderately motivated states, and the upper curve reflects neural function under highly aroused states. The slopes (right),

$$\frac{dQ}{dv} = \exp[v - (e^v - 1)/Q_m],$$

of these curves are bell-shaped and represent the neuronal gain at the trigger zones of neural populations. The small squares are the values at rest (P_o) in the absence of input. The maximal nonlinear gain is displaced to the excitatory side by $v_{gmax} = \ln(Q_m)$. Piecewise linearization is achieved by replacing the sigmoid with a straight line segment. From [16].

within a small-signal linear range, so that it is replaced by a scalar fixed gain, k_{ij} between the ith and jth populations. The three linear parts are collapsed into a single expression by combining $f_{a,i}$ in the presynaptic population with d_j and $f_{d,j}$ in the postsynaptic population. Then the expression for the operation of the jth population consists of a linear part, $F_j(s)$, in the complex operator $s = (\beta + \mathrm{j}2\pi f)$, and a static nonlinear part in dendritic wave density, $G_j(v)$. For any given domain of input and range of output the expression is linearized by replacing $G_j(v)$ with a scalar gain coefficient, k_{ij}, that includes d_{ij}, where i denotes the input population, and j denotes the output population. When $p_i(s)$ is the input and $p_j(s)$ is the output, then:

$$p_j(s)/p_i(s) = G_j(v_j)F_j(p_i)k_{ij}.$$

The common activity that is distributed over a substantial area of cortex is found to undergo both frequency modulation and amplitude modulation continuously at all times. However, when the amplitude can be controlled within relatively narrow ranges, experimentally we have shown by the use of superposition that small-signal linearity holds [1,5]. Over a set of domains of input amplitude we have found that the static nonlinear dynamics imposed by the sigmoid curve is subject to description by use of multiple near-linear domains. This approach is especially useful for describing the results of impulse driving of the cortex by means of electrical stimulation. In practice the coefficients in the linear transfer function and the terms to which they attach are fixed, and the nonlinear effects on the system of changing any variable that can alter the frequencies of the output are expressed in describing functions. These have the general form of a gain coefficient that is a function of an input variable such as stimulus intensity or of an output variable such as a measure of the amplitude of induced neural activity [4,15,19].

As is predicted for a negative feedback loop, the basic form of the impulse response is a damped cosine. Its amplitude is a monotonic function of the strength of the impulse input. Its phase is fixed for any fixed amplitude of input, unless the synaptic strengths of the interactions in the masses are modified by learning [7,15]. The phase and frequency of oscillation and decay rate of the envelope all change with changes in stimulus intensity [15]. The relationships are complex and require further detailed analysis for explanation.

2.5 Modeling with the Root Locus Technique

The fitting of a damped cosine to an oscillatory impulse response recorded from the cortex on electrical stimulation constitutes an instance of piecewise linearization. The frequency and the decay rate together serve to estimate a conjugate pair of complex roots of a linear differential equation that approximates the small signal linear dynamics of the system under impulse driving.

Because the complex roots change in small steps on making arbitrarily small steps in the stimulus intensity, each root traces a path in the complex plane that is known as a root locus as a function of input or output amplitude.

Root loci are also generated experimentally by various other techniques including using drugs to modify neural excitability, manipulating behavior involving learning, and varying the electrical bias under which the cortex operates by use of imposed electrical fields of transcortical current [23].

The greatest value of the root locus technique lies in testing models of the neurodynamics of the cortex using piecewise linearization. When a set of coupled linear differential equations is solved repeatedly for successively incremented values of the gain coefficients in its couplings, the complex roots of the solutions trace root loci in the complex plane, which can be compared directly with experimental loci, in order to determine whether a proposed model of cortical dynamics is admissible.

3 Linear Models of Cortical Feedback

3.1 Comparison of 1st and 2nd Order Kernels for Neuron Pools

The strengths of action of groups of neurons onto each other in feedback loops are variable in respect to learning, attention, motivation, and other behavioral variables relating to brain function, so it is important to be able to evaluate them. It is not possible to measure them directly in experimental work. Instead we measure the rate constants of the groups of neurons in the noninteractive "open loop state", which we induce in animals by suppressing brain function with anesthetics, and we then measure the closed loop rate constants. In order to estimate the closed loop gains, we must have a dynamic model of the feedback process. This is provided by the use of linear differential equations and the root locus technique, in which the time constants are fixed at experimentally derived values, and the strengths of action between and within pools of neurons are expressed as feedback gains, K_j.

As an example we begin with a hypothetical system, in which the neuron pool (a collection of neurons working in parallel with common input) is (abstractly) assumed to have an impulse response with an infinite rise time and an exponential decay. The dynamics is described by a first order linear differential equation

$$\frac{dv}{dt} + av = a\partial(t),$$

which, for the impulse input $\partial(t)$ (the Dirac delta function) gives the solution

$$v(t) = ae^{-at}.$$

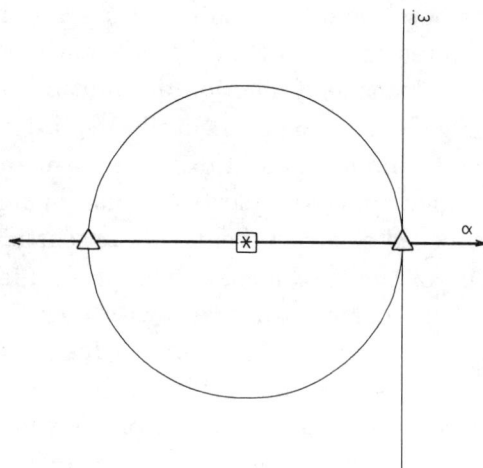

Figure 2:
The real and imaginary axes of the complex plane are shown near the origin. A double open loop pole is indicated by the asterix on the negative real axis. The small enclosing rectangle designates the location of a closed loop zero. The heavy lines show the two root loci starting at the two poles, and the arrows indicate the direction of increasing gain. The large circle is the isocontour for unity gain, and the small triangles at the intersection with the root loci show the locations of the two closed loop poles for positive feedback. The pole at the origin indicates the boundary of the region of stability to its left. From [15].

The Laplace transform using the complex operator s gives

$$v(s) = \frac{a}{(s+a)}.$$

When two first order elements are connected into a negative feedback loop with gain K, the closed loop equation in the operator s is

$$v(s) = \frac{a(s+a)}{(s+a)^2 - a^2 K}.$$

The denominator is expanded and factored to determine the closed loop roots. If the gain K is positive, the two roots have real values that depend on K. If K is negative, the real part is equal to a, and the imaginary part is equal to the frequency in radians/second. An example of the root loci for positive feedback is shown in Figure 2. The loop is stable for values of $K < 1$, and it is monotonically unstable for $K > 1$, with a step response for impulse input at $K = 1$. For negative feedback (Figure 3) the impulse response is oscillatory for $K > 0$ with fixed decay rate a, and the frequency increases monotonically with K. The loop is stable for all values of K.

The root loci for feedback between two second order elements differ in one crucial aspect. The complex root loci for negative feedback cross into

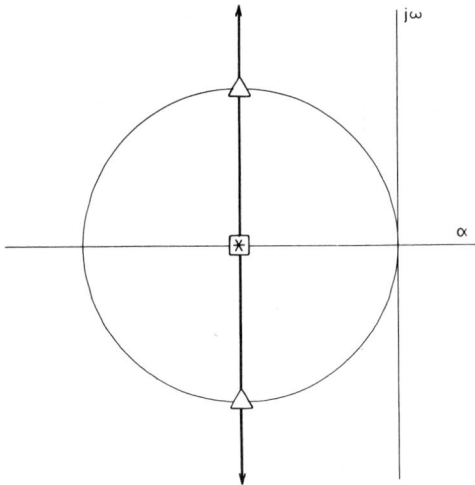

Figure 3:
The same conventions hold as in Figure 2, but the root loci are for negative feedback, and the closed loop roots form a complex conjugate pair. The frequency is proportional to the feedback gain, and the decay rate is fixed. The loop is stable for all values of gain. From [15].

the right half of the s-plane, showing that the feedback loop can be unstable in the oscillatory mode.

A second order linear differential equation is required to describe the impulse response that has a finite rise time (Figure 4), and thereby to approximate the form of the impulse response (postsynaptic potential) of single neurons and of noninteractive neuronal pools. The equation is:

$$\frac{d^2v}{dt^2} + (a+b)\frac{dv}{dt} + (ab)v = ab\partial(t)$$

in which b is the rate of rise in 1/sec and aD is the passive decay rate in 1/sec, and $\partial(t)$ is the Dirac delta function. The Laplace Transform gives

$$v(s) = \frac{ab}{(s+a)(s+b)}.$$

The closed loop equation for two elements in feedback with gain K is

$$V(s) = \frac{(ab)^2(s+a)(s+b)}{[(s+a)(s+b)]^2 - (ab)^2 K},$$

the denominator of which is factored to give the closed loop roots.

The root loci for the case of positive feedback (Figure 5) show that for $K < 1$ the loop is again stable, but for $K > 1$, it goes unstable monotonically as one root crosses into the right half of the s-plane on the real axis. In the case of negative feedback (Figure 6) the system goes unstable in the oscillatory mode for a value of gain near $K = 3.2$, but for lower values of K the impulse response is a damped cosine function.

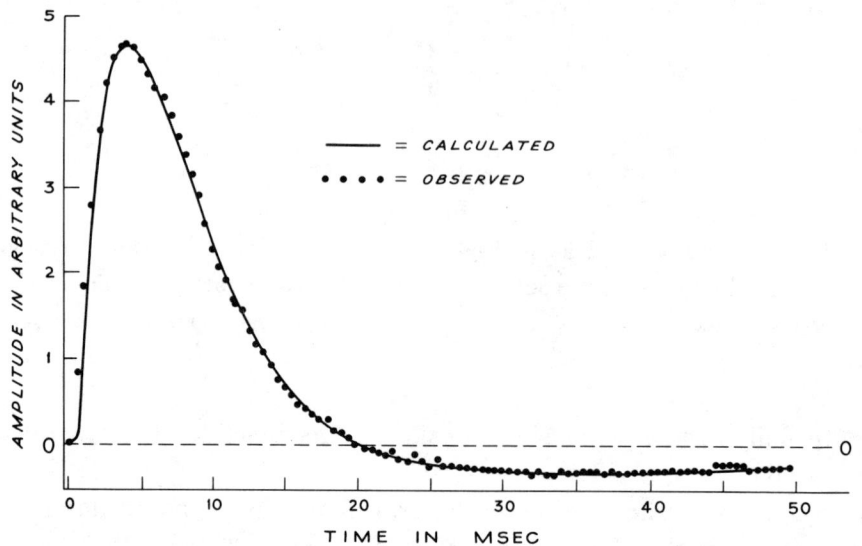

Figure 4:
The impulse response of a neural population that is in a non-interactive, "open loop" state (solid dots) consists of an average or "compound" postsynaptic potential (PSP) in an extracellular recording. A fitted curve consisting of a sum of exponential terms must have at least two terms to represent the finite rates of rise (dendritic synaptic delay) and of decay (the passive RC membrane property). Hence the dynamics requires at least a second order linear differential equation. From [4].

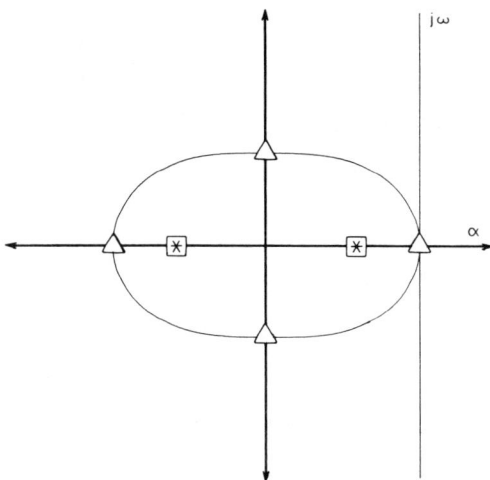

Figure 5:
Positive feedback between two neural populations with representation of each by a second order equation gives two double poles on the negative real axis and two real zeroes. One pair of root loci follows the real axis, and the other pair runs parallel to the imaginary axis. The isocontour for gain K_j intersects the origin and gives a pair of complex poles as well. The impulse response is a step function. If $K_j > 1$ the loop is monotonically unstable in the linearized model. The neural system is stabilized by its nonlinear gain. From [15].

3.2 Treatment of Multiple Coexisting Neuronal Feedback Loops

Feedback loops arise in three ways in the cerebral cortex. An example of a simpler form of cortex is taken from the olfactory bulb, which has an outer layer of sensory axons and external interneurons (the periglomerular cells - P or PG), and an inner layer of internal interneurons (the granule cells - G or GR) and projection neurons (the mitral and tufted cells - MT), which send their axons to the next succeeding layer of cortex in the olfactory system (Figure 7). A schematic diagram of their connections is given in Figure 8, which shows the three main types of feedback connection. Excitatory neurons (+) transmit to inhibitory neurons (−) and also receive from them so as to form negative feedback loops. Excitatory neurons (+)(+) that act on and receive from each other form positive feedback loops, which are also known as cooperative interactions. Positive feedback is also formed by mutually inhibitory neurons (−)(−), the best known example being the network of interconnecting inhibitory neurons in the eye of Limulus, the horseshoe crab, which constitutes competitive interaction leading to contrast enhancement.

These 3 types of feedback coexist in cerebral cortex, because excitatory neurons (**e**) transmit both to other excitatory neurons (**ee**) and to inhibitory neurons (**ei**), and likewise inhibitory neurons (**i**) send both to other inhibitory

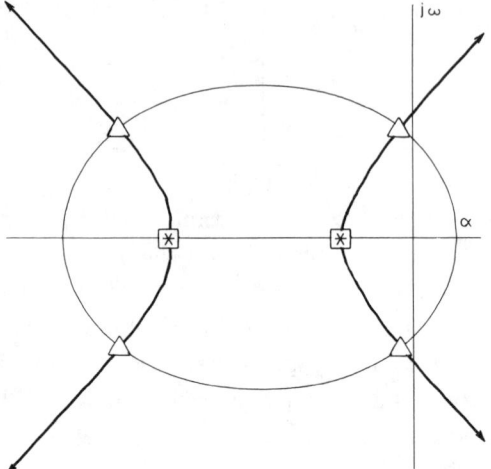

Figure 6:
Negative feedback between two neural populations yields two pairs of complex conjugate poles. One pair of root loci crosses the imaginary axis at a gain (not shown) of $K_n \approx 3.2$, at which the impulse response is a cosine of fixed amplitude. For $K_n > 3.2$ the loop is unstable in the oscillatory mode. For $0 < K_n < 3.2$ the impulse response is a damped cosine at the output of the forward limb. The output of the feedback limb is a damped sine. Owing to the nearly 90 degrees of phase lead contributed by the two closed loop zeroes, the oscillation of the forward limb leads that of the feedback limb by a quarter cycle of phase. From [15].

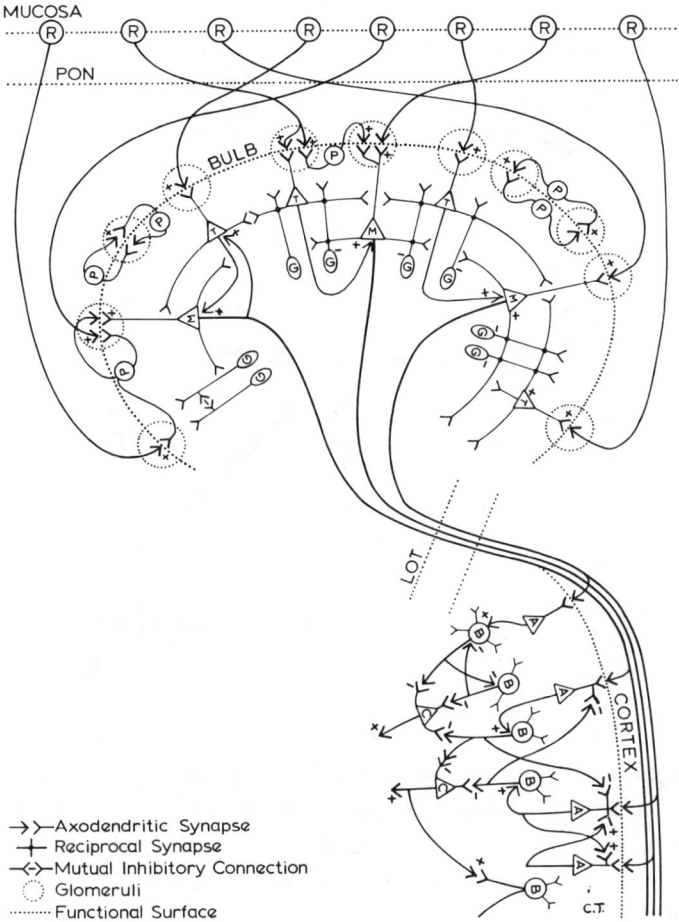

Figure 7:
A schematic diagram is used to show the principal cell types, pathways, and synaptic connections of the olfactory mucosa (receptors), bulb and prepyriform cortex. The primary olfactory nerve (PON) gives orthodromic input to the bulb from receptors, and the lateral olfactory tract (LOT) provides the bulb with its output path and an antidromic input path for electrically evoked stimuli. From [9].

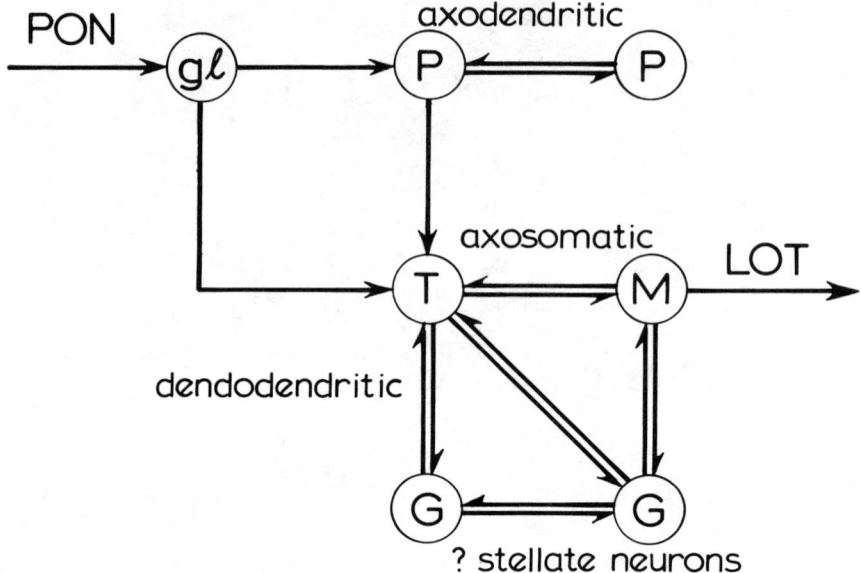

Figure 8:
The anatomical description of the bulbar connections as shown in Figure 7 is re-expressed in a circuit diagram. The outer bulb is formed by synaptic nests called glomeruli, in which receptor axons end on mitral-tufted (MT) dendrites and on periglomerular cell (PG) dendrites. The PG cells excite each other so as to form a positive feedback loop; they also attenuate the effectiveness of receptor input in a form of what is called "presynaptic inhibition," and they excite MT cells. The MT cells excite each other (positive feedback) and the internal interneurons, the granule cells (GR). The GR cells inhibit each other (again, positive feedback, possibly through the short-axon or stellate cells) and the MT cells (negative feedback). The MT cells provide the output of the bulb. The types of synapse are identified, and the signs of action are indicated by + (excitatory) and − (inhibitory).

neurons (**ii**) and to excitatory neurons (**ie**). It is useful therefore to describe four types of forward gain as k_{ee}, k_{ei}, k_{ie}, and k_{ii} and three types of feedback gain that the forward gains are used to define:

(1) $$K_e = k_{ee}k_{ee}$$
(2) $$K_i = k_{ii}k_{ii}$$
(3) $$K_n = k_{ei}k_{ie}.$$

Each of these forward and feedback gains is strongly influenced by the amplitude of neural activity due to the static amplitude-dependent nonlinearity in both of its connection pathways. The gains are interrelated with each other through the effects of sustained inputs to the cortical system, which have the roles of providing excitatory and inhibitory biases to the networks. Empirically a bias term ∂ is usefully defined as follows [15]:

(4) $$K_e = K_n(K_n^{\partial}K_o),$$
(5) $$K_i = K_n(K_n^{-\partial}K_o).$$

On the one hand, when $\partial = 1$, then $K_e = K_n^2/K_o$, and K_i is fixed at K_o. On the other hand when $\partial = -1$, then $K_i = K_n^2/K_o$, and K_e is fixed at K_o. Hence the term ∂ is particularly useful to describe the effects of excitatory and inhibitory biases on the operations of cortical networks, as will be seen in the next two sections.

4 Experimental Root Loci from the Olfactory Bulb

4.1 Local Circuits Representing Networks of Neural Populations

The olfactory bulb is a specialized region of cerebral cortex (Figure 7) that receives in its surface a massively parallel projection of axons from olfactory receptors in the nose. It transmits its output likewise in parallel by an array of axons coming from all parts of the bulb. Neural interactions in the bulb take place by axonal connections that run helter-skelter tangentially to the surface in all directions. Three main bulbar subpopulations have been characterized, one in the outer bulb called periglomerular (PG) cells, and two others in the inner bulb, one excitatory (the mitral-tufted or MT cells) and the other inhibitory (the granule or GR cells).

Artificial input is provided by electrical stimulation, which provides an impulse input with each electrical stimulus. There are two routes of access. The first is called orthodromic stimulation of the input pathway to the bulb, the primary olfactory nerve (PON). A volley of evoked action potentials is delivered to both PG and MT cells but not to GR cells. The second is called antidromic stimulation, because the electric shocks are delivered to the output pathway of the bulb, the lateral olfactory tract (LOT), so that action potentials propagate from the stimulus site both orthodromically in the direction of normal transmission to the prepyriform cortex, and back to the bulb antidromically in opposition to the normal direction of axonal transmission.

According to substantial evidence [10,11,12,13,32,33] the PG cells are excited by receptor axonal input, and they excite each other as well as MT cells (Figure 8). They do not transmit directly to nor receive from granule cells, so that they are neither excited nor inhibited by antidromic impulse driving of the LOT. Their impulse response consists of a rapid rise in their activity above the baseline of so-called "spontaneous" discharge and then a monotonic decay back to that baseline without overshoot (Figure 9). The rate of decay is monotonically related to the strength of stimulation and to the peak amplitude of responding [12].

Analysis of a linear model using the root locus technique shows (Figure 10) that the decay rate increases with increasing amplitude because of blocking or saturation in the feedback pathway between the PG cells, which is expressed by the sigmoid nonlinearity that controls their firing frequencies. On extrapolation to zero amplitude the response decay rate goes to zero. This implies that the PG cells maintain their "spontaneous" firing by mutual excitation, which is stabilized by the nonlinearity in their axonal firing mechanism [13,17]. There is no necessity for stabilization by inhibitory feedback, nor do their response properties indicate that direct inhibition occurs, although they are subject to an indirect form of response attenuation that has been mistakenly called "presynaptic inhibition" [10,11].

The orthodromic volley of action potentials that is evoked by the stimulus given to the PON also excites the MT cells. These respond with their own volley of action potentials that excite the granule cells (GR, Figure 11, upper right frame). The GR cells feed back with inhibition that suppresses the firing of MT cells. They quickly recover with another burst of firing followed by inhibition, then a third burst, and so on, each firing weaker than the last, so that the impulse response has the form of a damped cosine wave.

4.2 The Roles of Background Activity and Excitatory Bias

How does this happen? The answer is that both the MT and GR cells are normally active continually in basal so-called "spontaneous" firing. External perturbation drives them above that level. The GR cell inhibition suppresses the MT cells below that level, and because the GR cells fail to receive expected input, they are disexcited, and they disinhibit the MT cells, which then are re-excited. However, re-excitation requires some source of the sustained basal activity in order that the next cycle be initiated. Experimental

COLLIGATION OF CORTICAL OSCILLATORS

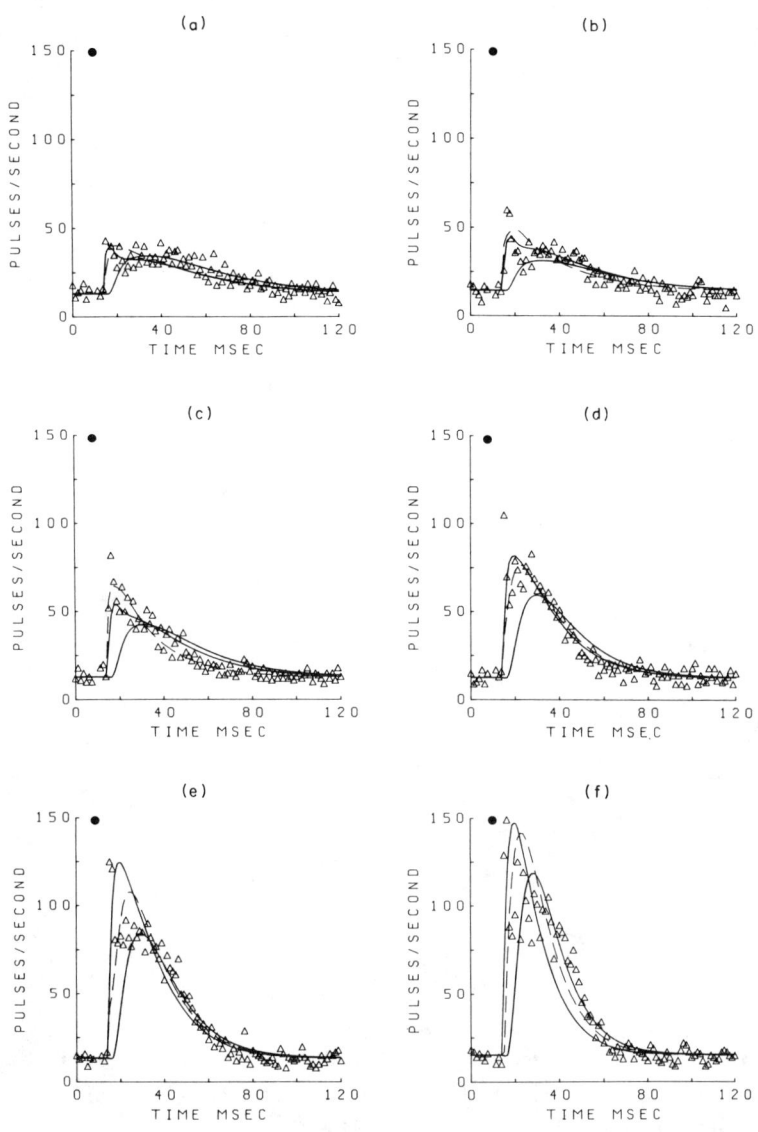

Figure 9:
The impulse response of the PG cells shows a rapid rise to a peak in firing rate and a monotonic decay to the basal so-called "spontaneous" firing rate. The decay rate increases with increased stimulus intensity owing to reduction of the loop gain by saturation, that increases with response amplitude. The solid fitted curves show the responses of the forward and feedback limbs, defined by those PG cells that directly receive the input and those that do not, and the mean output is shown by the dashed curve. With decreasing input strength the decay rate extrapolates to zero (step response) at zero input, implying that the steady-state background firing results from self-stabilized re-excitation within the interactive neural population. From [12].

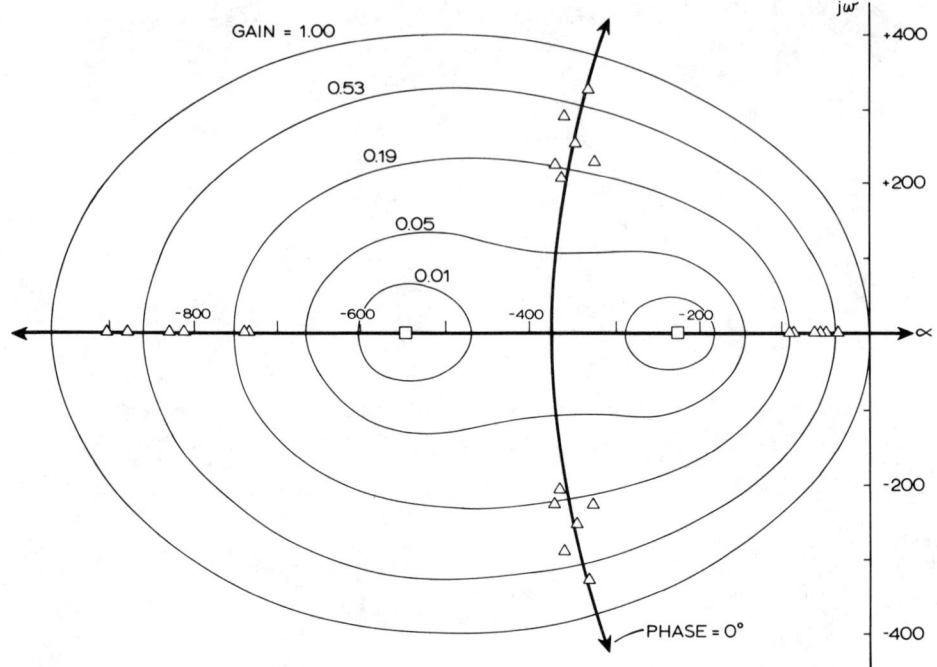

Figure 10:
The closed loop roots that were experimentally measured as shown in Figure 9 by curve fitting are plotted in the s-plane. The values for the closed loop zeroes (small rectangles) are estimated by trial and error for the best fit, and from the resulting fourth-order differential equation the root loci and gain contours are constructed as shown. The intercepts of the gain contours with the root loci give theoretical closed loop poles. Conversely, the experimental closed loop poles serve by extrapolation to estimate the closed loop gains. From [13].

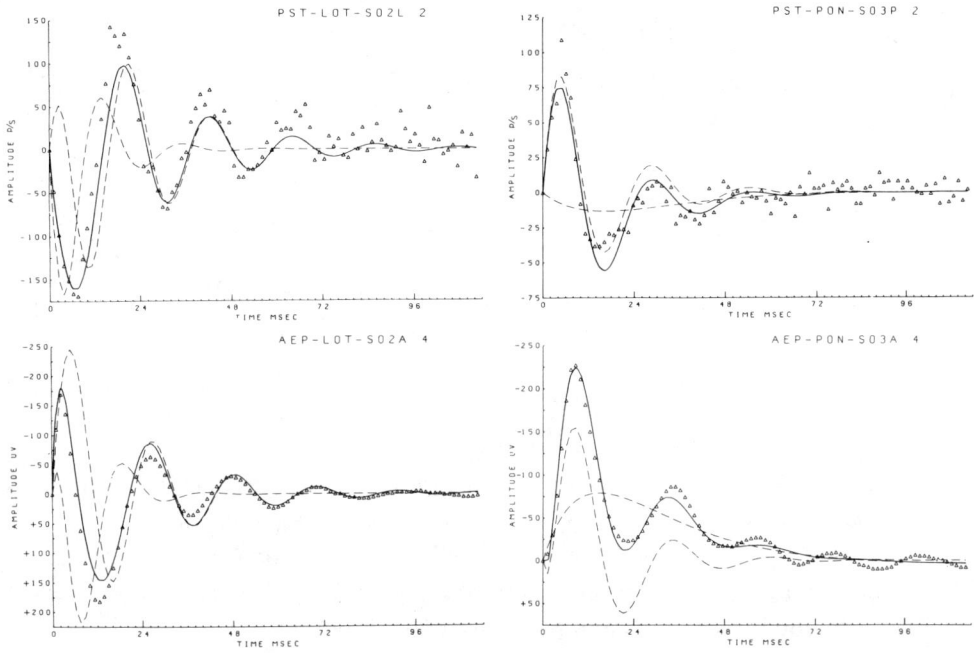

Figure 11:
The impulse responses of the bulb are shown for the MT cells (upper frames, the forward limb) and the GR cells (lower frames, the feedback limb), in response to orthodromic (PON) electrical stimulation (right frames) and to antidromic (LOT) electrical stimulation (left frames). The MT and GR outputs oscillate at the same frequency and decay rate in each pair, and the MT output leads the GR oscillation by a quarter cycle on the average as predicted (Figure 6). The PON response shows an upward baseline shift (right lower frame) that is absent in the LOT response (left lower frame). It is attributed to PG activation by PON input with monotonic PG activity (Figure 9), that is transmitted through the MT cells. The MT cells do not show this baseline shift (right upper frame) due to the closed loop zeros in the forward limb of the negative feedback loop (Figure 6) as explained in [32]. From [8].

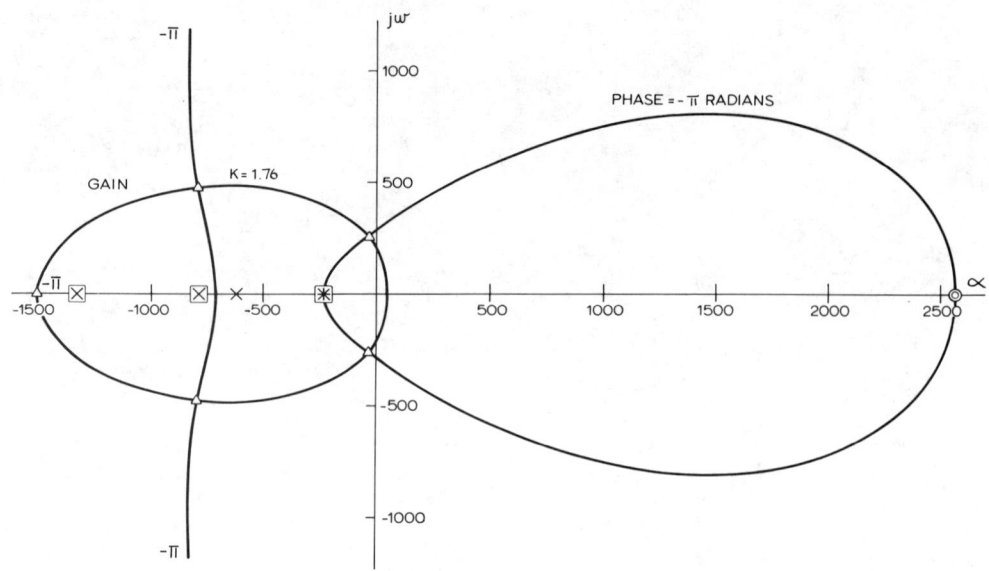

Figure 12:
A simplified root locus plot is shown in its entirety for the negative feedback interaction between excitatory (forward) and inhibitory (feedback) limbs between two neural populations. In subsequent figures only the upper half of the s-plane near the origin is shown, which contains the root locus of the pole corresponding to the dominant damped cosine of the impulse response. From [8].

analysis by surgical dissection [15] shows that the source of the excitation lies within the bulb, and that it is provided at least in part by the PG cells because of their own mutual excitation.

When the background activity of the bulb and of the prepyriform cortex (Figure 7) is suppressed by pharmacological or surgical procedures, their impulse responses become non-oscillatory. These "open loop" responses (Figure 4) are measured by fitting to them the sum of exponential curves, so as to derive estimates of the open loop rate constants of the generating neurons [15].

Experimental analysis has demonstrated that these rate constants are invariant over a wide range of conditions, including those of electrical impulse stimulation and also of behavioral information management. This verification enables us to plot them as fixed points in the left half of the s-plane on the negative real axis (Figure 12), and then to construct root locus plots for the closed loop case. When the closed loop rate constants are measured as complex conjugates by fitting sums of damped cosines and exponential terms to the oscillatory impulse responses (Figure 11), the closed loop negative feedback gain, K_n, can be evaluated from the root locus plot (Figure 12). Of course, in the open loop state, $K_n = 0$.

Evidence for the excitatory input of PG cells to MT cells is seen in Figure 11 (lower frames) by comparing the impulse response of the GR cells on PON input with that on LOT input. The PON stimulus excites the PG cells, which respond with an abrupt increase in activity followed by a monotonic decay to their basal level (Figure 9). This surge of activity is transmitted through the MT cells to the GR cells, as manifested by the baseline shift in the oscillatory impulse response of the GR cells that is initiated by the PON input impulse (Figure 11, lower right). This baseline shift in GR output is not seen on LOT stimulation, which activates the MT-GR feedback loop but not the PG cells (Figure 11, lower left).

The question arises, how is it that the output of MT cells does not show a comparable baseline shift on PON activation (Figure 11, upper right), even though the MT cells provide the sole synaptic link from the PG cells to the GR cells? The answer is that the MT cells are excited by the PG cells with the activity shown in Figure 9, but the MT response is counteracted by the surge of inhibition from the GR cells that is shown by the baseline shift in Figure 11, lower right. In the root locus plot (Figure 12) it is indicated that the open loop poles of the feedback loop become zeroes in the closed loop transfer function. The suppression (and in some instances the reversal in sign as in Figure 11, upper right frame) of the baseline shift of the MT cells is explained by pole-zero cancellation [15,30].

5 Theoretical Root Loci for Multiple Feedback Loops

5.1 Analysis of Effects of Isolated Changes in Forward Gains

The results thus far are summarized in Figure 13. The simplest level of dynamics is ascribed to a non-interactive population of neurons, which is denoted a K0 set. Its impulse response provides for experimental evaluation of the open loop rate constants of the population. A population such as the PG cells that interacts within itself by mutual excitation is denoted as a KI_e set, and its impulse response shows monotonic decay at a rate inversely dependent on the excitatory feedback gain K_e. This holds also for the MT population. The interaction of mutual inhibition holds for a set denoted by KI_i, of which an example is the population of GR cells. The impulse response is monotonic, but with opposing sign for the outputs of the forward and feedback limbs. Oscillations dominate with the interaction of excitatory and inhibitory neuron populations. The combination of negative feedback with the two kinds of positive feedback is denoted as a KII set, with the three kinds of feedback defined as K_n, K_e, and K_i in Section 3 by equations (1) to (3). When $K_e = |K_i|$, the two positive feedback loops cancel their effects, and the set becomes a reduced KII set.

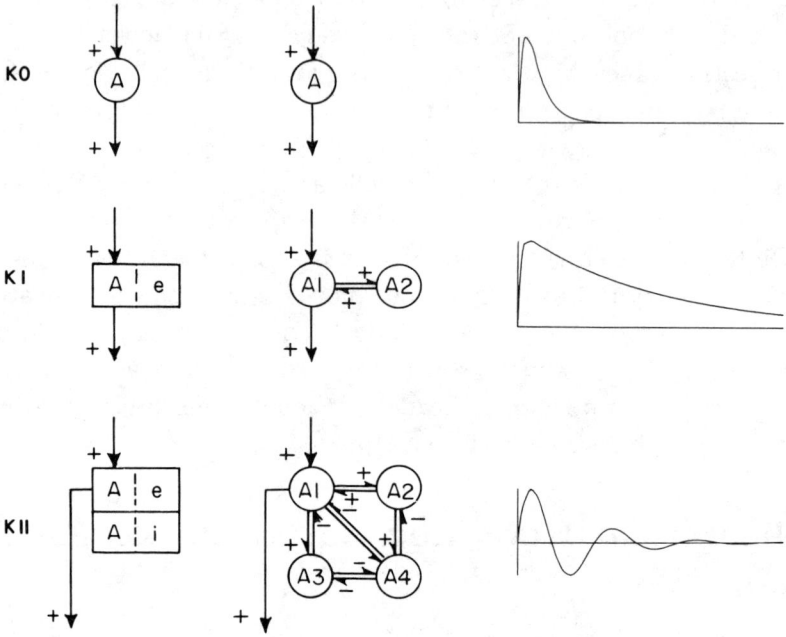

Figure 13:
A summary diagram reviews the hierarchy of neural populations and the forms of their impulse responses. The noninteractive population is denoted a K0 set, and it gives the open loop response. The interactive set such as the PG cells is denoted a KI set, and its impulse response is monotonic. The interaction of excitatory and inhibitory KI sets forms a KII set, and its impulse response is oscillatory. From [15].

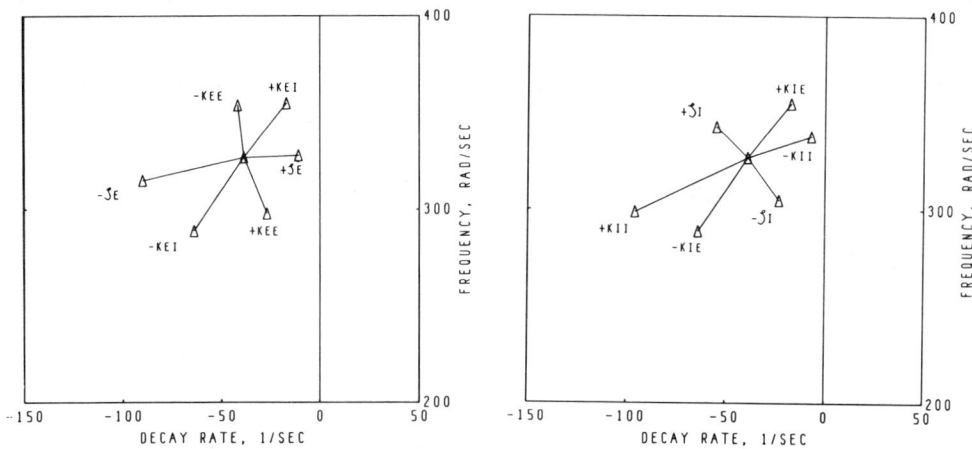

Figure 14:
A change in each of the four forward gains gives rise to a characteristic change in the frequency and decay rate of the impulse response of a network of excitatory and inhibitory neurons forming the three kinds of feedback loops. A schematic diagram is shown in Figure 13 (KII) of the multiple interconnections. This figure shows the complex root loci in the upper half of the s-plane near the origin, for a convenient value of the gains in a case of symmetry, that is, $K_n = K_e = K_i = 2.0$, which yields the frequency and decay rate shown by the small triangle in the center of each diagram. The effects on frequency and decay rate of a 10% increase or decrease in each of the forward gains are indicated for k_{ee}, k_{ei}, k_{ie}, and k_{ii}, and for the combinations k_{ee}, & k_ei and k_{ie} & k_{ii}.

For purposes of heuristic evaluation of the full KII set it is convenient to adopt a central point that is close to the frequency and decay rate of the typical physiological impulse response, and to set $K_n = K_e = K_i = K_o = 2.0$ (Figure 14). Then the effect can be predicted of making an isolated increase or decrease of 10% in each of the four types of forward gain, k_{ee}, k_{ei}, k_{ie}, and k_{ii}, and combinations of them, K_n, K_e, and K_i, to show the direction and magnitude of change in the frequency and decay rate of the impulse response. Two among these changes are of particular interest to behaviorists. One is an increase in k_{ee} that is identified to occur in associative learning, and the other one is a concomitant decrease in both k_{ee} and k_{ei} (that is, K_e) with habituation [7,15,17]. Other changes have been identified with various pharmacological effects.

For present purposes the most important change in gains and in the impulse responses is that which occurs with increasing stimulus intensity. As shown by an example in Figure 15, the cause of the changes in gains and in waveforms lies in saturation of the feedback pathways by driving response

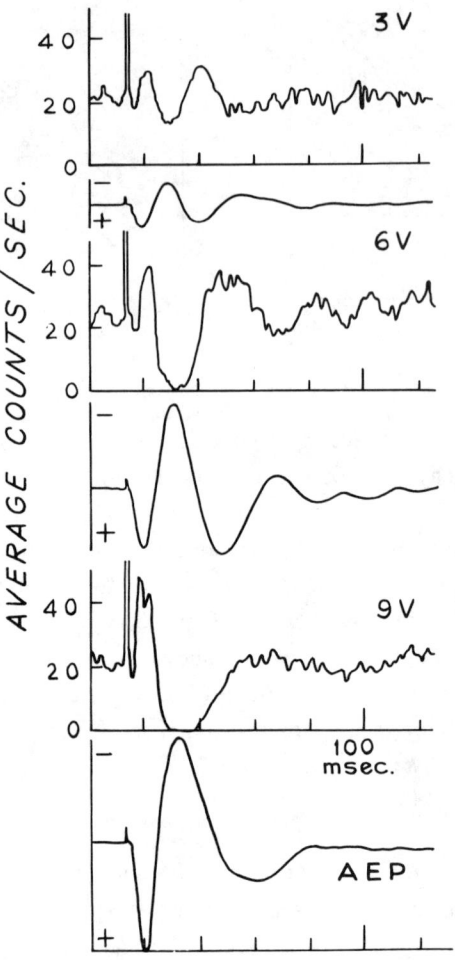

Figure 15:
Concomitant recordings are shown from the unit activity of an excitatory neuron in the prepyriform cortex (upper traces) and the local dendritic field potential (lower traces) from the depth of the cortex (accounting for its inversion in polarity). With increasing stimulus intensity the waveforms of the poststimulus time histogram (PSTH) and averaged evoked potential (AEP) decrease in frequency together. The cause is the saturation at zero firing rate during the inhibitory phase of the oscillation by the forward limb of the negative feedback loop. From [6].

amplitude during inhibition beyond the background level of pulse activity. Impulse driving is not limited by the excitatory response of the neurons. It is limited by the extent to which inhibition can be effected on and expressed by the neurons in the loop. If the neurons are inhibited to the point where their background activity is completely suppressed, then further inhibition cannot be expressed by the pulse train output. In effect, the system meets a limit stop. It is saturated. The effects of the saturation on the impulse responses can be expressed by reductions in feedback gains within the closed loop set.

5.2 Combining the Effects to Model Amplitude-dependent Changes

The phenomenon is complicated by the facts that three kinds of neural feedback co-exist, and that the relative amounts of reduction among the three depend on whether an excitatory bias is present by virtue of PG activation through the PON, or is not present by driving through the LOT. The resolution of this dynamic complexity is provided by using the bias parameter ∂, which is defined in Section 3 by equations (4) and (5).

Examples of the experimentally derived impulse responses are shown in Figure 16 for PON input (left frame) and LOT input (right frame) by the plotting symbols. The data have been fitted with damped cosines by use of nonlinear regression [15]. These changes in waveform are continuous with respect to stimulus intensity, because the amount of change is proportional to the size of increment of intensity of any amount. There is neither hysteresis nor time variance, because the order in which values occur does not depend on the order in which the input intensities are selected, although for small increments the changes are obscured by noise and errors of measurement. Each response in a series from the same stimulus site and animal can always be fitted with a curve from the same equation, consisting of the sum of damped cosines and exponentials. Thereby the changes in waveform with input amplitude can be expressed by sets of real and complex exponentials.

The frequency and the decay rate of the dominant damped cosine fix a pair of complex conjugate poles in the left half of the s-plane. A sequence of these poles determines an experimental root locus for input amplitude and response amplitude. Examples of such root loci are shown in Figure 17 by sets of small triangular plotting symbols. Only the root locus in the upper half of the s-plane is shown, because its conjugate is symmetrically disposed in the lower half. The direction of increasing input and output amplitudes is shown by the arrows. The downward locus on the left is from LOT input, and that on the right is from PON input. Whereas the response frequency decreases markedly with increasing LOT input amplitude, it does not change significantly with increasing PON input.

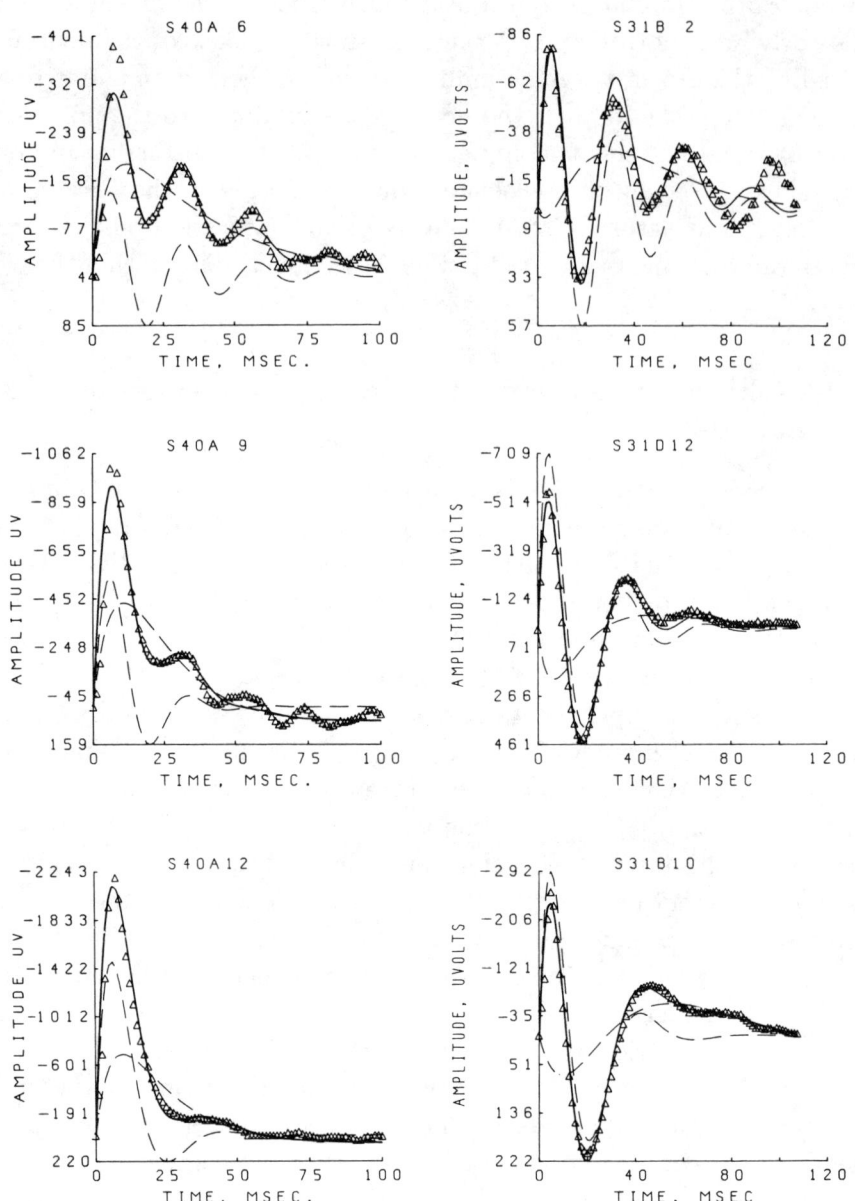

Figure 16:
The AEPs from the bulb behave differently with increasing stimulus intensity, depending on the site of stimulation. The impulse at near constant decay rate, whereas those on PON input (left frames) which have the PG-induced baseline excitatory shift show constant frequency and increasing decay rate of the fitted damped cosine. From [15].

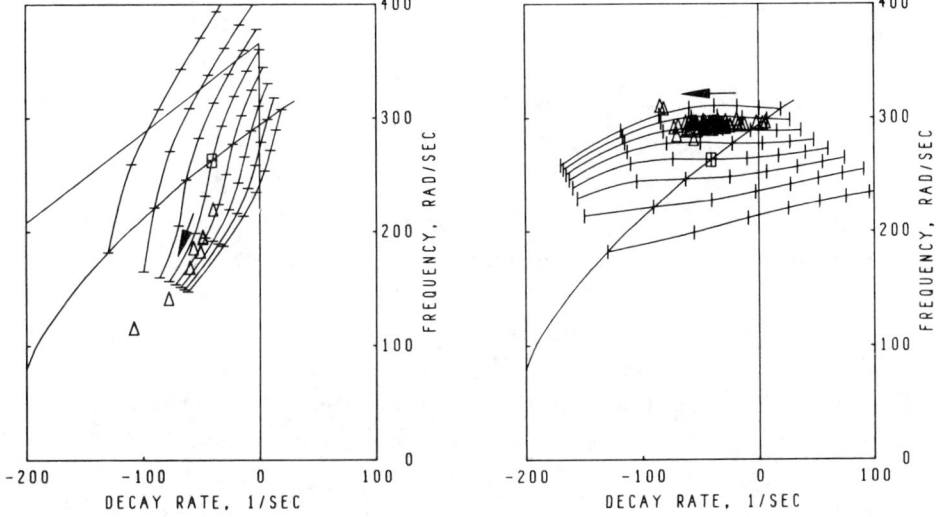

Figure 17:
The poles of a set of bulbar responses to LOT input with increasing stimulus intensity (arrow) show decreasing frequency (left frame), whereas the poles of a set of responses to PON input show constant frequency and increasing decay rate (right frame). Theoretical root loci are calculated to derive estimates of the closed loop gains, K_n, K_e and K_i, for the two sets, as described in the text. From [15].

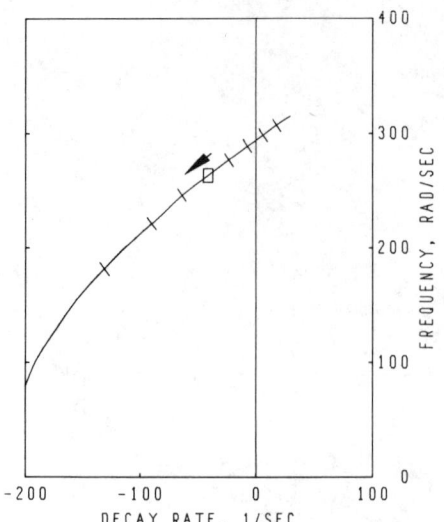 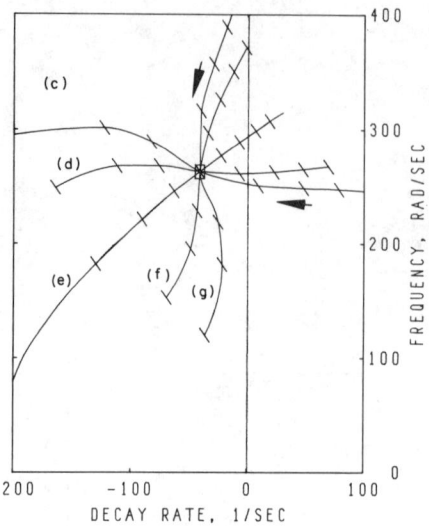

Figure 18:
The left frame shows the root locus for a KII set in which $K_n = K_e = K_i$ for all values of K_n. The steps are for gain changes of 0.5, the rectangle shows $K_n = K_o = 2.0$, and the arrow shows the direction of decreasing K_n (increasing saturation). This locus is rarely seen experimentally, implying that the symmetry constraint does not hold. The right frame shows the root loci that result from fixing $K_o = 2.0$ and varying the bias parameter ∂ (see the defining equations in Section 3). The effect of fixing K_o and and ∂ at other values is displayed in the families of curves with varying K_n in Figure 17 for $\partial = 0.4$ (right frame) and $\partial = -0.4$ (left frame). From [15].

Theoretical root loci are constructed to fit these and other experimental root loci by use of the parameter ∂ as defined by equation (4) in Section 3 (see also Freeman, 1975, Chapter 5). When $\partial > 0$, the KII set has a positive (excitatory) bias by which $K_e > |K_i|$. Conversely when $\partial < 0$ the KII set has a negative (inhibitory) bias by which $|K_i| > K_e$. In Figure 18 (left frame) $\partial = 0$. The value of K_o is set to 2.0 (the small rectangular plotting symbol in Figures 17 and 18), so that variation of K_n in steps of 0.1 defines a theoretical root locus for decreasing K_n (direction of the arrow), which occurs with increasing amplitude owing to saturation (Figure 15).

The procedure is repeated for $K_o = 2.0$ and different values of ∂ as indicated in Figure 18 (right frame) to obtain a family of root loci in ∂. Finally, the procedure is repeated for selected values of K_o at each value of ∂ to derive the families of curves shown in Figure 17. The selection of the closest fitting theoretical root locus depends on the values chosen for K_o and ∂ and the closest point on the curve to an experimental point gives an estimate for the closed loop gain K_n. The values for K_e and K_i are

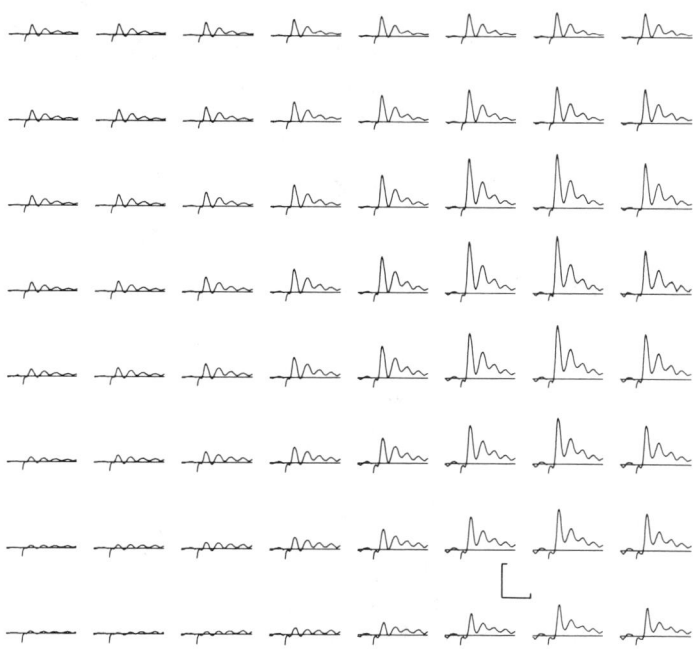

Figure 19:
A set of 64 AEPs is recorded simultaneously from an 8 x 8 array of electrodes spaced 0.5 mm apart. The electrical stimulus evokes an input that is maximal near the center of the induced focus and decreases in all directions outwardly. The result is unequal response amplitudes. Yet the frequency of the evoked oscillation is everywhere the same (see Figure 17, right frame). From [14].

then calculated by equations (4) and (5) in Section 3. This completes the evaluation of the closed loop feedback gains from the closed loop frequencies. Thereby the dominance of K_e is shown for PON input and of K_i for LOT input in determining forms of bulbar impulse responses.

5.3 Comparison of Experimental and Theoretical Root Loci

The significance of this result is shown in Figure 19, which displays a field of evoked potential averaged and recorded concomitantly from an 8 x 8 array of 64 electrodes. The frequencies and decay rates of the fitted curves are plotted in the right frame of Figure 17, demonstrating that the frequency is independent of response amplitude owing to the variation of input intensity spatially. This is in contrast to the variation in response frequency and amplitude that occurs with LOT input, as shown by three sets of 4 simultaneously recorded and averaged evoked potentials from 4 sites separated by 1 mm over the field of the response to electrical stimulation (Figure 20). The variation in frequency is seen at all stimulus intensities. The downward shift

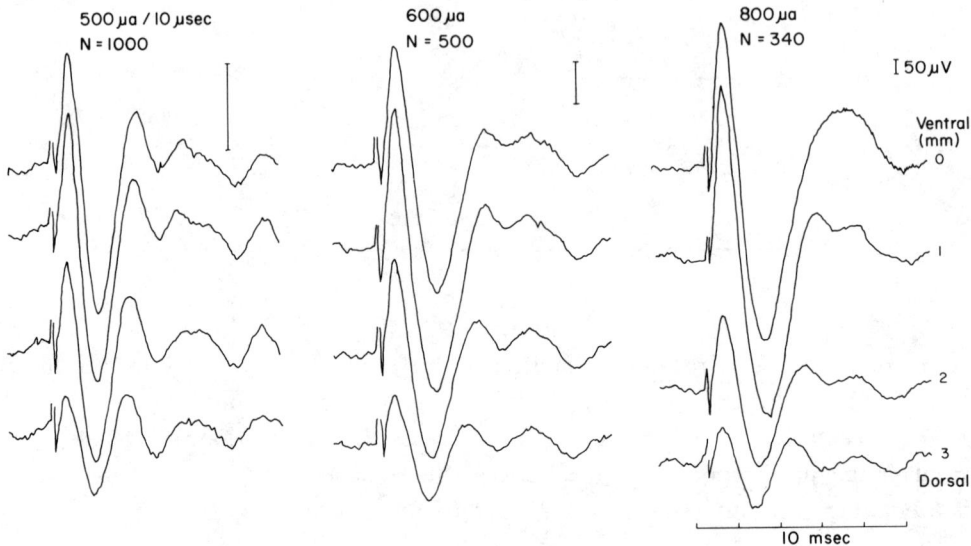

Figure 20:
Four AEPs are simultaneously taken from sites spaced 1.0 mm apart on the bulb at three intensities of LOT electrical stimulation. The impulse responses show that there is not a common frequency of oscillation over the bulb for any input intensity. From [15].

in frequency with increased input and output amplitudes is reflected from a similar set of data with fitted curves, yielding the points shown in Figure 17 (left frame).

These data show that a significant contribution of the PG cells that are coactivated by PON input is to collapse the distribution of the characteristic frequencies of bulbar oscillation so as to make them independent of input amplitude, thereby to enable a common frequency of oscillation to emerge across the entire array of stimulated elements in response to unevenly distributed input and despite the spatially inhomogeneous output.

6 Discussion

Recordings of the oscillatory activity of the bulb and the prepyriform cortex (Figure 7) made simultaneously from up to 64 electrodes placed on the surface show that there is a common instantaneous frequency of the oscillations at all times, despite continuous variation in the common frequency over time [28]. Behavioral information is expressed in spatial patterns of amplitude modulation of the common waveform or "carrier" in the rabbit olfactory system [25], in the somatosensory cortex of the human [26], and in the visual cortex of the rhesus monkey [27]. The mechanism for readout of the information by real-time spatial integration [21] requires that there be a common instantaneous frequency, yet the frequency of oscillation is shown to be strongly influenced by the amplitude of oscillation. Therefore, a mechanism must be sought that provides compensation for the effects of amplitude variation on frequency, in order that amplitude modulation might readily occur at the common frequency.

The results described here show that the requisite compensatory effect is provided in the olfactory system by an excitatory bias that is evoked by input and accompanies the input stimulus into the oscillatory system. A similar mechanism may exist in the somatosensory system at the level of the spinal cord, by the neurons of the substantia gelatinosa generating the slow dorsal root potential [35]. The bulbar and prepyriform mechanisms also depend on synaptic and dendritic cable delays to provide the required stability properties, such that an excitatory input surge tends to destabilize the cortex rather than to change its frequency. This is an important aspect of burst formation, in which a state transition occurs when the cortex is destabilized by an input-dependent gain increase [19], which leads to the expression of perceptual information by the cortex [34].

There are two implications for design of neurodynamic models based on coupled oscillators for pattern formation and classification. (a) Enhancement of input-dependent state changes can be achieved by using a second order differential equation as the kernel of integration, rather than the most commonly used first order equation; and (b) the provision of a generic excitatory bias that is triggered by input may be crucial for the convergence of frequencies of oscillation to a common mode, when strong local variation in amplitude is required for the expression of functional information.

Examples of these principles of operation for pattern classification are shown in several published reports [18,24,29,3,36,37].

References

[1] Biedenbach, M. A. and Freeman, W. J. "Linear domain of potential from the prepyriform cortex with respect to stimulus parameters," *Experimental Neurology*, **11**, 400-417, 1965.

[2] Eeckman, F. A. and Freeman, W. J. "Correlations between unit firing and EEG in the rat olfactory system," *Brain Research*, in press, 1990.

[3] Eisenberg, J., Freeman, W. J. and Burke, B. "Hardware architecture of a neural network model simulating pattern recognition by the olfactory bulb," *Neural Networks*, **2**, 315-325, 1989.

[4] Freeman, W. J. "A linear distributed feedback model for prepyriform cortex," *Experimental Neurology*, **10**, 525-547, 1964.

[5] Freeman, W. J. "Analysis of function of cerebral cortex by use of control systems theory," *The Logistics Review*, **3**, 5-40, 1967.

[6] Freeman, W. J. "Relations between unit activity and evoked potential in prepyriform cortex of cats," *Journal of Neurophysiology*, **31**, 1-13, 1968.

[7] Freeman, W. J. "Analog simulation of prepyriform cortex in the cat," *Mathematical Bioscience*, **2**, 181-190, 1968.

[8] Freeman, W. J. "Measurement of oscillatory responses to electrical stimulation in olfactory bulb of cat," *Journal of Neurophysiology*, **35**, 762-779, 1972.

[9] Freeman, W. J. "Waves, pulses, and the theory of neural masses," *Progress in Theoretical Biology*, **2**, 87-165, 1972.

[10] Freeman, W. J. "Attenuation of transmission through glomeruli of olfactory bulb on paired shock stimulation," *Brain Research*, **65**, 77-90, 1974.

[11] Freeman, W. J. "Relation of glomerular neuronal activity to glomerular transmission attenuation," *Brain Research*, **65**, 91-107, 1974.

[12] Freeman, W. J. "A model for mutual excitation in a neuron population in olfactory bulb," *Transactions IEEE Biomedical Engineering*, **21**, 350-358, 1974.

[13] Freeman, W. J. "Stability characteristics of positive feedback in a neural population," *Transactions IEEE Biomedical Engineering*, **21**, 358-364, 1974.

[14] Freeman, W. J. "Topographic organization of primary olfactory nerve in cat and rabbit as shown by evoked potentials," *Electroencephalography and clinical Neurophysiology*, **36**, 33-45, 1974.

[15] Freeman, W. J. *Mass Action in the Nervous System*, Academic Press, New York, 1975.

[16] Freeman, W. J. "Nonlinear gain mediating cortical stimulus-response relations," *Biological Cybernetics*, **35**, 237-247, 1979.

[17] Freeman, W. J. "Nonlinear dynamics of paleocortex manifested in the olfactory EEG," *Biological Cybernetics*, **35**, 21-37, 1979.

[18] Freeman, W. J. "EEG analysis gives model of neuronal template-matching mechanism for sensory search with olfactory bulb," *Biological Cybernetics*, **35**, 221-234, 1979.

[19] Freeman, W. J. "Techniques used in the search for the physiological basis of the EEG," in *Handbook of Electroencephalography and clinical Neurophysiology*, Gevins, A., and Remond, A., (eds), **3A**, Part 2, Ch. 18, Amsterdam, Elsevier, 1987.

[20] Freeman, W. J. "Simulation of chaotic EEG patterns with a dynamic model of the olfactory system," *Biological Cybernetics*, **56**, 139-150, 1987.

[21] Freeman, W. J. "On the problem of anomalous dispersion in chaoto-chaotic phase transitions of neural masses, and its significance for the management of perceptual information in brains," in *Synergetics of Cognition*, Haken, H. and Stadler, M. (eds), Springer, Berlin, 1990.

[22] Freeman, W. J. and Baird, B. "Relation of olfactory EEG to behavior: Spatial analysis," *Behavioral Neuroscience*, **101**, 393-408, 1987.

[23] Freeman, W. J. and Baird, B. "Effects of applied electric current fields on cortical neural activity," in *Neurocomputation*, E. Schwartz (ed.) New York, Plenum, 1990. Pages 378-389.

[24] Freeman, W. J., Eisenberg, J. and Burke, B. "Hardware simulation of brain dynamics in learning: the SPOCK," *Proceedings IEEE First Annual Conference on Neural Networks*, **III**, 435-442, 1987.

[25] Freeman, W. J. and Grajski, K. A. "Relation of olfactory EEG to behavior: Factor analysis," *Behavioral Neuroscience*, **101**, 766-777, 1987.

[26] Freeman, W. J. and Maurer, K. "Advances in brain theory give new directions to the use of the technologies of brain mapping in behavioral studies," in *Topographic Mapping of EEG and Evoked Potentials*, Maurer, K. (ed.), Springer-Verlag, Berlin, 1989.

[27] Freeman, W. J. and Van Dijk, B. "Spatial patterns of visual cortical fast EEG during conditioned reflex in a rhesus monkey," *Brain Research*, **422**, 267-276, 1987.

[28] Freeman, W. J. and Viana Di Prisco, G. "Relation of olfactory EEG to behavior: Time series analysis," *Behavioral Neuroscience*, **100**, 753-763, 1986.

[29] Freeman, W. J., Yong Yao, and Burke, B. "Central pattern generating and recognizing in olfactory bulb: A correlation learning rule," *Neural Networks*, **1**, 277-288, 1988.

[30] Gonzalez-Estrada, T. M. and Freeman, W. J. " Effects of carnosine on olfactory bulb EEG, evoked potentials, and D.C. potentials," *Brain Research*, **202**, 373-386, 1980.

[31] Llinas, R. R. "The intrinsic electrophysiological properties of mammalian neurons: Insights into central nervous system function," *Science*, **242**, 1654-1664, 1988.

[32] Martinez, D. M. and Freeman, W. J. "Periglomerular cell action on mitral cell in olfactory bulb shown by current source density analysis," *Brain Research*, **308**, 223-233, 1984.

[33] Rhoades, B. K. and Freeman, W. J. "GABAergic modulation of EEG and evoked potentials in the rat olfactory bulb," *Abstracts, American Chemosensory Society*, in press, 1990.

[34] Skarda, C. A. and Freeman, W. J. "How brains make chaos in order to make sense of the world," *Brain and Behavioral Sciences*, **10**, 161-195, 1987.

[35] Wall, P. D. "The origin of a spinal-cord slow potential," *Journal of Physiology*, **164**, 508-526, 1962.

[36] Yao, Y. and Freeman, W. J. "Models of biological pattern recognition with spatially chaotic dynamics," *Neural Networks*, in press, 1990.

[37] Yao, Y., Freeman, W. J., Burke, B. and Yang, Q. "Pattern recognition by a distributed neural network: An industrial application," *Neural Networks*, submitted, 1990.

Chapter 6
Directions in Natural Language Processing[*]

Mitchell Marcus[†]

1 Introduction

Twenty years from now, researchers in natural language processing will look back at the early 1990s as a major watershed in the development of powerful natural language understanding systems. The prevalent paradigm of the last twenty years is now giving way to new paradigms which center on robust processing of unconstrained text using technologies built upon the automatic acquisition of linguistic structure. This shift in paradigm is unavoidable, because the majority of research efforts, particularly in the U.S., have focused on only one small part of the problem of natural language understanding by machine.

1.1 The Ultimate Goal

The major goal of natural language processing is to build machines that understand and produce both spoken and written language at least as well and as appropriately as people do. For tasks such as simultaneous translation, which good human translators can do for no more than a half hour at a time, one would certainly like machines with greater endurance than people. With respect to written language, the ultimate goal is to produce machines that can both read and write unconstrained text. Such machines should be able to abstract information automatically from unconstrained text such as newspapers or books, accurately retrieve information relevant to particular topics from an ongoing text stream, and summarize retrieved information into data bases of various kinds.

---

[*]This work was partially supported by DARPA grant No. N0014-85-K0018, by DARPA and AFOSR jointly under grant No. AFOSR-90-0066, and by ARO grant No. DAAL 03-89-C0031 PRI. Section 4.4 is adapted from Magerman[16]. Thanks to Eric Brill, Ken Church, Don Hindle, Dave Magerman and Lyle Ungar for discussion of issues included here.

[†]Department of Computer and Information Science, University of Pennsylvania.

Another goal is to develop systems that users can merely talk to, with speech input and output providing a transparent interface to a wide variety of systems. Certainly the major barrier preventing many individuals in many different settings from using computer systems now is that users are forced to approach the computer on the computer's own terms. Allowing users to interact with a computer system on the user's terms rather than the computer's is a prerequisite to natural and effective access to computer systems. Ultimately, it is necessary that we allow users to not only speak to computers, but that users be able to use informal everyday speech; this will be particularly challenging, given that essentially all speech recognition work until several years ago was based upon carefully read speech. Even in the short term, spoken language must be combined with graphic output and pointing devices such as mice in a rich multi-modal environment. And in both spoken and written language systems, we would also like to have automatic translation capabilities.[1]

These are the goals to which Natural Language Processing aspires. In the remainder of this paper, we will review the past of natural language processing, and then suggest that the near-term future of this field depends upon work that uncovers computational models which exploit the idiosyncratic behavior of the human language processing faculty, and, most crucially, is capable of acquiring linguistic structure from the automatic analysis of large corpora of natural language text.

2 The Past-Interactive Systems in Constrained Domains

2.1 SHRDLU

The focus of most research activity for the last twenty years, in the U.S. in particular, has been the development of interactive systems. These are systems which interact with a user in natural language, where the user can tailor his or her language to the limitations of the system. A good exemplar of early natural language understanding systems in this mold is Winograd's SHRDLU [22], constructed in the late sixties. This program pulled together for the first time natural language analysis and text generation with a simulated model of a robot and a simple reasoning system which sufficed to perform simple actions in a simulated world of children's blocks. It was a wonderful proof of concept for full-blown natural language understanding. The system's capabilities included the ability to understand utterances such as

---

[1]The above derives from an analysis of the aims and objectives of NLP in Weischedel [21]. This article, a DARPA white paper coauthored by the present writer, also provides an alternative consensus-based view of the near term future of natural language processing.

>(1) Will you please stack up both of the red blocks and either a green cube and a pyramid?

and to perform the requested actions. SHRDLU also had the ability to answer questions about the state of its simulated world, its past actions, and its reasons for doing those actions. On the other hand, SHRDLU worked only as long as the input sentences stayed fairly close to the particular scenario for which it had been debugged. Like many demonstration programs that followed it, the program itself was incredibly fragile. With time, it also became clear that the fundamental architecture of the program made SHRDLU extremely difficult to extend.

SHRDLU was capable of correctly dealing with many of the linguistic subtleties of our language which we usually fail to notice. For example, the form of sentence (1) is a question, although it functions not as a question, but as a command. The sentence fragment "Will you stack up" appears to begin a question about what the hearer is going to do in the future, just as one can ask "Will you go to the market sometime in the next week?" simply asking for information about the hearer's shopping plans. In everyday language, however, questions can serve as a polite way of making a request or giving an order. Here, of course, the "please" serves to clearly flag that this surface question is to be taken as a request and not as a literal question.

2.2 TQA

About ten years later, a group of researchers at IBM used an inverse form of Chomsky's early ideas about transformational grammar to build a question answering system called TQA (for Transformational Question Answering) that was used in a real application for a two year period with fair success [19]. The system was put into the town planning office of the town of White Plains, NY, and was the only way that two of the data bases used in that office could be accessed for the period of the experiment. During those two years, town planners input a wide range of sample sentences into the system. Examples include:

> Where are the parcels with a LUC of 641?
> What single family houses in Fisher Hill have exemptions greater than $0?
> How many two family houses are there in the Oak Ridge Residents Assn.?

Over the two year period, the system gave correct responses to over 85% of all of the sentences typed, including such sentences as "Who killed Cock Robin?", which were obviously input just to test the limits of the system. Perhaps more importantly, every attempt to extract some particular information from the data bases required at most three attempts (which was quite important, because the system took at least a minute on average to process a query). Somewhat more anecdotally, each month, the researchers would ask how the system might be improved; after six months the response was a request to put the system on the remainder of the data bases in the town planning office rather than spend the time improving the performance of the system.

This success story leads immediately to two questions: Why didn't the researchers do just that? Given this kind of success ten years ago, why aren't such systems in use everywhere today? The answer to both questions is that it has been estimated that this system and similar systems of about this period would require about 10-15 person-years to port to a different data base, i.e. a different set of facts imbedded in the same data base management system. Although it didn't appear to be so at the time, these systems wove together facts about the English language and the particulars of the application domain at hand in a very complex mesh.

Note that the example sentences given above aren't quite English; no one says "exemptions greater than 0 dollars" in either casual speech or formal writing. Given that TQA required such highly stylized English to function, how could people learn to use such a system? The answer - and this is key to much of what follows below - is that this entire technology depended upon a magical ability not of the AI software or the underlying hardware, but of people: *Given only a small set of exemplar sentences, people can magically adapt and limit their language to match the capabilities of the system they are speaking to automatically and almost without conscious effort.* This is true as long as the range of phenomena that the system handles can be characterized in certain ways which people find intuitively natural. A system which has this property is called a *habitable* system. A system is habitable if the subset of natural language it handles is in some sense natural with respect to the organization of our cognitive faculty for processing language. Unfortunately, we cannot formally characterize exactly what makes a system more or less habitable at the present time. If a person who had never used a particular system of this first generation of systems attempted to use it and go beyond the first cautious query or two, there was little chance that the system would be able to handle the query. But if one merely showed the prospective system user a list of example sentences which the system *can* handle, such as the list given above, they will have little difficulty staying within the limits of that system. This property of people is perhaps the single most important fact about most of the natural language processing technology (with some exceptions) until just a few years ago.

2.3 NLC

In another key experiment, Ballard and Biermann, then both at Duke University, invented a language called NLC (for Natural Language Computing) which allowed programming matrix operations in a limited and stylized sub-

```
Display a 4 by 5 matrix and call it testmat
Fill the matrix with random values.
Choose an entry and call it p.
Define a method to pivot testmat about p.
    Choose an entry not in the p row and not in the p
        column and call it q.
    Compute the product of the entry which corresponds to q
        in the p row and the entry which corresponds to q in
        the p column.
        ...
    ...
```

Figure 1:

A fragment of an NLC program.

set of mathematical English[1]. The NLC system had an initial vocabulary of about 200 words, although the user could define new words which stand for variables. Figure 1 gives a small fragment of an NLC program. To test the usefulness of designing programming languages that read like mathematical English, Ballard and Biermann asked a group of Duke undergraduates who had just completed a first course in programming using the PL/C language to solve problems in both PL/C and NLC. Although these students had only a 45 minute tutorial introduction to NLC, they solved these problems much more quickly in NLC than in PL/C, and with fewer residual bugs in the final code. It must be noted, of course, that there is a confounding factor here which somewhat clouds the results: NLC is a special purpose language for working on matrices, as a quick examination of the code fragment in Figure 1 will reveal. On the other hand, note that we as humans have invented a special mathematical sublanguage for talking about matrices and matrix operations, and NLC just exploits this property of natural language. One motivation for using English as an interaction language for computers is just this: we already have specialized and limited sublanguages for many of the technical tasks which we need to perform.

2.4   First-generation Commercial Systems

How could commercial natural language systems have been developed during this period, given the person-years of work to port data base front ends such as TQA to new applications? The solution was to develop products which actually used extensions of key-wordlike techniques to analyze language. These systems appeared to perform a full fine-grained analysis of the

List everyone hired since 1/1/83.

```
Create a report showing
  the Full name and
  the Department and
  the Hired date from the forms on which
  the Hired date is on or after 1 Jan 1983.
```

Show me the salaries in each division, with totals for each division.

```
Create a report showing
  the Department and
  the Full name and
  the Salary
      with total from ALL forms sorted by
    alphabetical Department.
```

Figure 2:

Some examples of queries to Q&A.

grammatical and semantic fine-grained structure of language input to them, but in fact worked otherwise, as we will see below. Figure 2 shows some sample outputs from one such system, taken from the first version of Q&A, developed by Symantec, Inc. for IBM PCs and compatibles. Very similar techniques were used in systems which provided natural language front ends for DBMSs which ran on IBM mainframes, but which marketed for tens of thousands of dollars. (Q&A 3.0, the current version, uses a rather different and much better technology. It currently costs under $250 a copy, at street prices.)

Perhaps not surprisingly, these systems necessarily fail on certain kinds of inputs. So, if Q&A 1.0 is asked "Is everyone in legal female?" and there is one woman in legal, it will incorrectly answer yes. If asked "Show salary averages for all men and all women." Q&A 1.0 will just give the salary average for everyone, perhaps not surprisingly. If asked "What is Johnson's manager's salary," it will show information about Johnson, including Johnson's salary and Johnson's manager's name, which is incorrect, but which will allow the user, with one more query, to determine Johnson's manager's salary. As a final example, the query "Show employees who manage salespeople" will give a list of all managers and salespeople. These failures are intrinsic to the way this and similar systems worked; to counter this problem, this and similar systems always show the user the system's analysis of each query and ask whether the query has been correctly understood. On the other hand, these

Translation when style is closely matched:

> By using the 2-dimensional numerical simulation of planar vacuum arcs, effects of self-consistent magnetic fields to arc plasma density, temperatures and heat flow are obtained.

Translation when style is badly matched:

> Simple methods by operating conditions of wide ranges it operates by simple methods by single DC power sources two arcs are shown.

Figure 3:

Two examples of the output of Japanese to English machine translation.

limitations prove quite habitable; users of these systems quickly learn their limitations and simply avoid problematic cases. Systems that use essentially this technology are still sold quite widely.

2.5 Machine Translation

This whole first generation of systems, from TQA to Q&A, depended crucially upon the magical fact that people change their behavior to match the system's abilities. The key exceptions to this trend were the few systems which had to deal with preexisting unconstrained texts on their own terms. Perhaps the best of these, at least in terms of robustness, have been systems for automatic machine translation. One of the best machine translation (MT) systems is the University of Kyoto system which translates engineering abstracts from Japanese into English. The performance of this system has been very carefully studied and documented, with Nagao [18] providing a statistical characterization of the intelligibility and semantic accuracy of a range of translations.

However, while this system and other advanced MT systems often work quite well, the underlying technology is extremely style-sensitive. If the style of the input document closely matches the implicit expectations of the system, the translation is usually quite good, as in the first sample shown in Figure 3. If the style seriously violates the assumptions of the system, as happens at least occasionally, the translation can be quite terrible, as the second sample in Figure 3 demonstrates.

This current generation of MT systems are based on what are called *transfer dictionaries*. These systems work by doing an analysis of the grammar of the source language, yielding a parse tree in the source language. The transfer dictionary tells how to map subtrees for particular lexical items in the source language into the corresponding syntax subtrees in the target language. A transfer system thus maps a parse tree in the source language into a parse tree in the target language, which is then converted into a grammatical word string by a conventional language generation program. This leads to the immediate problem, however, that to translate from any of n languages into any of the other $n-1$, one needs n^2 translation systems. There is some leverage to be gained by having built a range of similar systems, but there is also much work to be done per language pair.

The obvious best-of-all-possible-worlds solution would be to find some kind of interlingua, a representation language, say, into which all source languages could be translated, and from which every target language could be generated. This would allow n analyzers and n generators to be combined into n^2 analyzers with no intervention. Some work is now going on toward such a goal, but the problem is extremely difficult, appearing to require something like a fundamental understanding of the semantic representation of all of the subtleties of human language.

3 The Present: First Attempts at Unconstrained Text

In many ways, there are really two fundamentally different natural language understanding technologies at the moment: one for interactive systems and the other for noninteractive systems. Interactive systems have depended very heavily on that fact that they need only handle constrained language, given the magical adaptation of users to machines. Within the United States, in particular, almost all work outside of machine translation has been within this paradigm, at least until the last few years. In both Japan and Europe, the need for automatic or semiautomatic translation has forced researchers to deal with unconstrained text in a noninteractive mode. And while a range of such machine translation systems now exist, all of these systems work within particular limited domains most of which have highly stylized lexicons and limited, highly conventional grammars; the language of these domains are often called *sublanguages*. The task is made somewhat easier for some of these sublanguages, in that much of the information is in long strings of noun-noun modifiers (e.g. "directory management tools"); a dictionary of these strings can do much of the work of translation.

It appears to be very difficult to build systems that actually understand unconstrained preexisting texts except in domains that either have highly conventionalized sublanguages or that are guaranteed to have highly stereotypical messages. For example a system has been developed by Cognitive Systems, Inc. that successfully extracts the relevant information from interbank telexes for transfer of funds between accounts. From each message, the program extracts five pieces of information: the originating bank and the destination, the account numbers at both banks, the sum to be transferred, and a control number for that transaction. The system successfully extracts about 85-90% of this information, with an extremely low level of false information.

Recently, a major shift of research paradigm has taken place, as typified by key differences between two Message Understanding Conferences called MUCK I and MUCK II, both sponsored by the Defense Advanced Research Projects Agency (DARPA) of the U.S. Department of Defense. Each of these conferences was really a competition at which message understanding systems were tested on previously unseen messages in a common domain to which all the systems had been ported. (Both were conducted on messages in highly telegraphic sublanguages in tactical military domains.) These conferences were held only two years apart, yet differed enormously in task and success rate. Before the first conference, the paradigm was to take a set of ten or twenty reports, and develop a system which could pull every bit of meaning out of that handful of reports, and then extend the system's coverage to handle another dozen reports. These systems essentially tried to use the same paradigms as constrained, interactive systems. Without automatic human adaptation to their weaknesses, however, they were both fragile and limited. The competition consisted of being given both a new set of messages to handle and a few days in which to make necessary extensions and alterations. Even so, most systems did rather poorly. By the second round, the paradigm had begun to change; system builders had finally begun to take seriously the very different requirements of processing unconstrained text. Here, hundreds of training messages were provided, with tens of test messages, and these messages were processed entirely blind. Despite this strict requirement, the best systems determined the five most important parts of each message about 80% of the time.

Within the last year, several prototype systems have been developed to extract information from maintenance reports of one kind or another. Specific applications have varied from domains such as jet engine failures to new car warranty service for engine stalls. Although quite different in design, these systems uniformly fill in about 70% of the fields in data base records correctly when tested on randomly selected new messages. These data base fields summarize such information as what failed, the cause of failure, and the maintenance action taken. The development of systems capable of acceptable robust behavior on unconstrained input within a fixed domain signals a significant advance.

4 The Future

4.1 Cognitively-tuned Processing Models

What will it take to go from 70% correct for the domain of engine stalls to 98% correct in the unrestricted domain of warranty maintenance? This section will focus on one part of the problem, that of building syntactic analyzers capable of parsing unconstrained text.

For the last eight or ten years, it has often been claimed that parsing, the best understood aspect of natural language processing, is a solved problem. Many researchers appear to believe that automatic grammatical analysis of the front page of the New York Times or the Associated Press newswire, say, is a solved problem. But in fact, nothing could be further from the truth. In an informal study of a number of so-called large-coverage parsers conducted recently by a well-known researcher in a related field, the best parser currently available in the United States could parse correctly only 60% of sentences under 13 words in length taken from an unconstrained sample of English text, while most others parsed well under 50% correctly. This study confirms the impressions of many of the top researchers in automatic grammatical analysis. Parsers have been developed which work very well within tightly constrained subdomains, and these parsers can often be rapidly moved (in a few person-months) to new applications in similar domains. The language in all of these domains, however, appears to be limited to highly constrained sublanguages characterized by the statistical predominance of a fairly limited set of stock constructions, a limited vocabulary and a highly consistent style.

What will be required to build parsers which *are* capable of parsing the New York Times? First of all, any successful research program must take the particulars of language very seriously. It must deeply utilize what theoretical linguists have to tell us is special and idiosyncratic about human language, and then use computational mechanisms which are closely tailored to these properties of human language. Two examples, both taken from the work of Don Hindle, a researcher at AT&T Bell Laboratories are discussed in the next two subsections.

4.1.1 Deterministic Parsing

As of the late seventies, researchers widely believed that because of the inherent rampant ambiguity of natural language, determining the correct grammatical analysis of even a simple sentence potentially required a search through a large combinatoric set of possibilities. The author's own thesis work [17] went against this belief by suggesting that a parsing mechanism with a very particular architecture could eliminate this combinatoric search. This work proposed a parser which had a small buffer which enabled the parser to hold on to several completed chunks of grammatical structure before it decided the role of the first of them. This allowed the parser to utilize a bounded amount of right context, as well as the entire previous left context, before determining the role of each constituent in the sentence. This parser was presented as a cognitive model, a model of the operation of the processing and analysis of grammatical structure within the human mind, the step in language understanding between deciding what words are in the input speech or text stream and deciding what those words mean in that particular order and particular context. This work proposed the hypothesis (termed the *determinism hypothesis*) that the grammatical structure of natural language could in fact be analyzed by a deterministic device which worked within a bounded amount of time per input item rather than exhibiting time behavior which was a higher order polynominal function (or worse an exponential) of the length of the input string.

The evidence from psycholinguistic experiments since that time has been mixed with respect to the correctness of this theory, and the jury is still out about this issue. Surprisingly, however, the parsing model proposed above has turned out to be an excellent engineering tool for developing highly capable natural language processing systems. Fiddithc, a parser developed by Hindle at the University of Pennsylvania and then extended at AT&T Bell Laboratories, is a deterministic parser along the lines described here which parses unconstrained text at a rate of about 30 words per second, and with a competitive success rate in the analysis of free text. Hindle's parser tends to parse about one sentence in three in free text completely without error, with about one error per sentence on average. However, when it does make an error, most of the remainder of the structure of the sentence on which the parser "failed" is correctly assigned, and the parser returns a string of fragments (almost all of which are correctly analyzed) whenever the full analysis process fails.

4.1.2 Self-correction of Fluent Speech

A second even more surprising result is that Hindle has developed a purely deterministic algorithm for correcting self-corrections in speech [13]. Casually spoken speech has many false starts and fluent self corrections, where the speaker will in essence edit out a word or two of the utterance. For example, a transcript of a taped description of this phenomenon (spoken by the author at the NEC Symposium which gave rise to this volume) reads as follows, where "–" marks a distinctly noticeable phonetic event where speech appears to be suddenly terminated, and then restart.

> "It – it turns out that when people – when people are talking, they – they'll often do what I'm – what I'm doing now; they'll – sit here and they'll begin to say – they'll decide to start a sentence a different way and they'll just – they'll correct their speech. And as a resu – We don't even notice it when people do

this unless somebody points it out when they're doing it."

Despite the apparent disfluency of the transcript, listeners barely notice the corrections, although they sense of lack of smoothness in the speech. About one quarter of all utterances in normal speech contain such fluent self corrections.

These fluent self-corrections would appear to undermine the very foundation of current speech recognition technology. Current approaches to the recognition of continuous speech depend crucially on exploiting the constraints imposed by very tightly constrained models of language production to limit the search space of possible words that the recognizer must seriously consider given likely candidates on purely phonetic grounds. These self corrections pose perhaps the worst possible problem to such search techniques; viewed purely formally, they would appear to impose the need for an exponential backward search for restart points if an overall grammatical analysis is to be derived and used to control lexical retrieval.

Hindle's algorithm correctly determines what material to edit out on over 97% of fluent self-corrections when tested on hundreds of sentences taken from socio-linguistic transcripts annotated in the same fashion as the transcript fragment above. Furthermore, the algorithm is purely deterministic and operates in linear time, running simultaneously with the parsing process itself. The fundamental rule used by Hindle's analyzer is simply that whenever the linguistic material before an instance of this phonetic editing signal is "the same thing" as the material immediately afterwards, then the material before is eliminated. Hindle's analyzer takes as "the same thing" two sequences of material that are either phonetically identical, or that are identically the same word, or that are complete or incomplete constituents of the same kind (e.g. a noun phrase, a verb phrase, a sentence). A secondary rule is that if one of a small set of special words like "oh" or "well" or several others immediately follows an edit signal, then completely restart the analysis of a sentence. If neither of these rules applies, then simply eliminate the editing signal; the speaker hesitated but decided to complete the utterance as it stood.

Note that the structure of this algorithm is closely tailored to the architecture for deterministic parsing discussed above. A small buffer of up to three linguistic constituents is exactly what is required to hold onto a first linguistic entity, the following edit signal, and a following linguistic entity which needs to be compared to the first.

4.2 Systems that Learn

To build highly capable natural language processing systems, we have no choice but to build systems that learn. Although this notion seems radical, it is true for many different reasons. First and foremost, it appears that the grammar of any given particular language contains just too many idiosyncratic facts to be able to exhaustively build such a grammar by hand. Secondly, dialect differences (e.g. that people from Pittsburgh, PA say "My hair needs washed" where the more widespread dialect requires "My hair needs to be washed") mean that a system will encounter subtle and not-so-subtle grammatical differences between different speakers. Without dialect studies far beyond the completeness of any yet undertaken, writers will be unable to take these differences into account. Also, the grammar of any living language is far from static; grammar changes with time in ways that are often unobserved by linguists. This means that any grammar, no matter how complete, will need to be modified at some constant rate either manually or automatically.

This kind of automatic learning no longer appears to be impossible. In this section, we will present some results from recent work in automatically trained methods to determine the lexical part of speech tag (i.e. whether a given word in a particular context is a noun or a verb) for unconstrained text, as well as some ongoing work in our research group in automatically determining the grammatical analysis of unconstrained text based on an automatic statistical analysis of a large corpus of material tagged with part of speech information.

4.2.1 Resolving Lexical Ambiguity

To see what the problem of lexical ambiguity is, consider the following pair of sentences, classic among researchers in natural language understanding:

(2a) Time flies like an arrow.
(2b) Fruit flies like a banana.

In sentence (2a) "flies" is a verb, while in sentence (2b) it is a noun. In (2a) "like" is an adverb, while in (2b) it is the main verb of the sentence. This kind of ambiguity is pervasive in English; an examination of the Brown corpus, a sample of one million words of written English, shows that over 40% of the words in this corpus are used in more than one part of speech. Note also that the ambiguity of various words in (2a) and (2b) is apparent to us only because of the juxtaposition of two differing interpretations. Despite the pervasive ambiguity of English, we are completely unaware of this problem most of the time. Somehow, contextual clues serve to allow us to automatically resolve such ambiguities without conscious effort.

Like the problem of fluent self correction in speech considered above, it initially appears that the phenomenon forces a potentially very expensive combinatoric search through the space of part-of-speech possibilities to resolve the correct interpretation of any particular sentence. Within the last few years, however, researchers have developed a variety of algorithms, all of which correctly determine the part of speech in context of more than 95%

of the word tokens in unconstrained text. All of these systems have been evaluated using a uniform set of criteria: First, each system was trained on the bulk of the text in the tagged Brown corpus [10], a million words of text collected from a variety of different text genres and styles, for which the part of speech of each word was carefully determined and checked by Kučera and Francis at Brown University by the end of the seventies. Second, each system tagged a reserved section of the untagged Brown corpus, text which it had never before encountered, and the percentage of tags assigned in the corresponding section of the tagged corpus which agreed with those originally assigned was computed.

The most accurate approach currently, due to Ken Church at Bell Labs [6], uses a purely stochastic technique. This tagger combines the statistical priors for part of speech distribution for each individual word type with the statistical distribution of the part-of-speech tags of every three word sequence in the training corpus. (Such triples might be "determiner noun verb" or "verb particle adverb.") The program has an error rate of under 2 1/2%, which is all the more remarkable given that the Brown corpus itself has a fair degree of inconsistent use of tags in many subtle although common cases, and the error metric is an exact match against that often inconsistent tag assignment. In contrast to this highly statistical approach, the deterministic parser described above, Fidditch, now uses a set of symbolic lexical disambiguation rules which were acquired by a fully automatic process. The acquisition process itself is primarily symbolic; the rules themselves are purely symbolic and are exactly of the same kind that Hindle's parser normally uses. The automatic rule acquisition system that resulted from this work [14] is quite a bit better than Hindle's hand developed set, with an error rate of under 3%, as determined by the same test discussed above. A connectionist approach due to Benello [2] has achieved somewhat lower performance, at about 5% overall error, although an examination of the published work makes it somewhat unclear if this error rate resulted from a test on previously reserved material.

It must be stressed that while these error rates look quite small when computed on the basis of error per word, they are in fact far too large for many purposes. An error rate of 2.5% error per word yields an error rate of about 40% per twenty word sentence, while an error rate of 5% per word yields an error rate of 65% per twenty word sentence. Although we clearly need to develop techniques which are robust in the face of a small number of errors per sentence for other reasons, we still need techniques which are much more accurate.

It is worth noting that all of these part-of-speech tagging systems, most surprisingly, are purely syntactic. It is often claimed that the only way to resolve the pernicious ambiguity of natural language is to utilize the detailed context of utterance of sentences, including the particulars of the real-world situation in which such sentences are uttered. Ultimately, perhaps this will prove true in general, and it is certainly true for such issues as prepositional phrase attachment (e.g. whether the prepositional phrase "in the park" in the sentence "I saw the man in the park." modifies just "the man", in which case I may not have been in the park, or the entire sentence, in which case the seeing event itself occurred in the park). It is surprising and encouraging that levels of performance this high have been achieved without resort to kinds of information which we, at present, do not know how to robustly code for more than very small closed domains. Just five years ago, no one would have guessed that performance levels this high could be achieved given just syntactic information.

4.3 Combining Nature and Nurture

These successes in automatic acquisition of linguistic structure strongly motivate a vigorous new research program to see how far the paradigm of trainable systems can take us towards the fully automatic analysis of unconstrained text. This work ought to proceed, we suggest, by attempting to combine two different traditions which have been viewed as mutually exclusive for the last thirty years: namely, the research program of generative grammar, as set forth originally by Noam Chomsky [4,5], and the research paradigm of distributional analysis, as developed by the American structural linguists resulting in the mathematical and computational work of Zellig Harris [11].

The theory of generative grammar is founded on the view that the essence of the linguistic structure which a child appears to acquire is in fact innate. It postulates that language learning is really just a process of selecting the correct grammar from a highly constrained set of enumerable language models. This paradigm has been the dominant paradigm for research in both competence linguistics and natural language understanding for almost thirty years. The notion of learning through distributional analysis, on the other hand, is that a child acquires its language through a bootstrapping procedure based upon a distributional analysis of the language which is spoken around it. Harris argues not only that the facts about any human language are discovered by the child from a distributional study of the structure of the language, but also that automatic techniques can be developed that emulate this process.

The core idea of generative grammar is undisputable true, given what we now know about the underlying structure of the apparent diversity of the world's languages. A small but key set of linguistic phenomena are very abstract; some of these phenomena are only observable in multiply embedded sentences, while others cause effects across long distances. These phenomena are very far from surface apparent; and it is very difficult to see how any child could derive these facts from any distributional analysis. Chomksy's view, that these generalizations are simply inherent in the human linguistic faculty, and are therefore universal to all human languages, appears to be supported by much evidence, and therefore provides an elegant solution to this learning problem.

The demonstration that such deep universal phenomena existed was enough to convince most linguists to abandon support for Harris's view in the sixties. Also, if this view were completely correct, then languages could potentially differ over a much wider range than has been observed; the only constraint ought to be that all relevant generalizations of each language should be determinable within the limits of the process of distributional analysis. But, as stated immediately above, this is not the case; there is a core of very abstract generalizations which are true of all languages and which appear to be anything but the consequences of some underlying distributional learner.

On the other hand, a full specification of the grammar of any particular natural language would appear to be extremely extensive. The reflex of the facts of universal grammar in such a document would be completely overwhelmed by a huge number of quite idiosyncratic, although quite superficial, language specific phenomena. The current best reference grammar of English [20] runs over 1500 pages, almost all of which is particular idiosyncratic facts usually focused on particular lexical items. These rules, it would appear, must be learned from the linguistic context by a child, and it seems quite plausible that a distributional analysis may provide the mechanism by which such rather local facts are learned.

Thus, it would seem that we must attempt to build language learning mechanisms which combine both nature and nurture, as it were, which add to a Chomskyean component of universal mechanisms another component which can learn facts about particular languages from a distributional analysis of the linguistic environment. Furthermore, it seems that the largely symbolic representation which serves as a basis for current theories of generative grammar is far from epiphenomenal, and that therefore forms of representation that can combine symbolic representations with distributional knowledge must be investigated. The author, for one, believes that a correct model of language acquisition will have an architecture which is quite different from anything which we quite imagine at present.

4.4 First Steps toward Distributional Analysis

We are now beginning to carry out this research program at the University of Pennsylvania, attempting to build different learning mechanisms based on both distributional and nativist models. One approach we are investigating is to see how much we can do using only distributional techniques, using a range of both unannotated and annotated text corpora as input, and discovering exactly how it is that this approach fails. At this point, we intend to investigate whether principles which are putatively true of all human languages are applicable in such a way that these principles solve the problem at hand. We believe that the result will be a largely distributional system which utilizes a few key facts of universal grammar. Given that universal grammar is postulated by current theories to be both very abstract and very small, this research proposal is far less in conflict with the program of generative grammar than may first appear to be the case. We are also pursuing the opposite approach in parallel, attempting to build a learner which contains a highly articulated view of the structure of Universal Grammar. We then intend to see what kind of language particular facts this approach fails to capture without tremendous ad-hoc extension of the form of UG, and ask whether distributional analysis techniques might suffice to acquire this residue.

While the second part of this research program is just beginning, research into distributional analysis has already yielded results which are both surprising and encouraging. For the past year, we have investigated how accurately the grammatical structure of a sentence can be determined using only distributional facts derived from a statistical examination of a corpus of text, without using an explicitly encoded grammar at all. We have simplified the problem for the moment by using the million-word tagged Brown corpus [10], a corpus of text with each word tagged for its part of speech in that context. A new kind of parser has emerged from this work which parses without an explicit grammar; it tabulates the statistics of part-of-speech tag sequences in the Brown corpus, and then uses this information to hierarchically subdivide new input text into smaller and smaller grammatical constituents. Since the information is derived entirely automatically from text which is not annotated for higher level grammatical structure, the parser indicates the subdivisions of the sentence in an *unlabeled* bracketing, since it has no basis on which to determine what labels it should use on those brackets. On a reserved test set containing text which was not part of the original statistical training, the parser misplaces about 2 to 3 brackets per sentence for sentences of length less than 15 words, and tends to misplace about 5 to 6 brackets on sentences from 30 to 60 words in length. In the end, of course, one needs to be able to generate an analyzer given only a corpus of text without part of speech annotation, and so we are concurrently experimenting with techniques to automatically derive a tag set for a corpus of text, again using only distributional facts. Initial results (reported in [3]) are very encouraging.

Our vision is essentially that of Zellig Harris', somewhat revised: Given a corpus in an undetermined natural language, we would like to ultimately have programs which can automatically determine a part of speech tag set for that language, tag the corpus with that tag set, and then use some statistical parsing technique to determine the grammatical structure of that corpus. In the end, we expect that constraints from Universal Grammar will need to be imposed on a purely distributional process to achieve this goal.

Our experiments to date are only the first small steps in a rather ambitious research program, but they are very encouraging nonetheless.

4.5 Parsing Using an Information Theoretic Measure

The statistical measure that we are exploiting is called *mutual information*, an information theoretic measure that has been explored over the last several years in a body of work both at IBM [15] and at Bell Labs [7,8]. Essentially, mutual information [9] is a measure of the extent to which one event can be used to predict another, of how much information the second event actually gives, given that the first event is already known to have occurred. The mutual information statistic is a function of the probabilities of the two events and the probability of their co-occurrence:

$$\mathcal{MI}(x,y) = \log \frac{\mathcal{P}_{X,Y}(x,y)}{\mathcal{P}_X(x)\mathcal{P}_Y(y)}$$

where $\mathcal{P}_{X,Y,}(x,y)$ is the probability over the cartesian product of the set of events X and Y of the particular pair of events x and y co-occurring. If x and y are completely independent of each other, then $\mathcal{P}_{X,Y}(x,y)$ is just $\mathcal{P}_X(x)\mathcal{P}_Y(y)$, so the ratio of numerator to denominator in the equation above is 1, and the log will be 0. If y only occurs after x and nowhere else, then $\mathcal{P}_{X,Y}(x,y)$ is identical to $\mathcal{P}_X(x)$, and the ratio is just $1/\mathcal{P}_Y(y)$, which will be quite large, given that $\mathcal{P}_Y(y)$ will be quite small for any real case of part-of-speech tags in natural language. If y is *negatively* correlated with x, then the ratio will be less than 1, and $\mathcal{MI}(x,y)$ will be negative. Figure 4 shows the analysis that this program gives for a typical input when it makes no errors; the syntactic labels shown next to each branching point are *not* produced by the program, but are given here so that the reader with some linguistic sophistication can see that the analysis is, in fact, correct. For this system, our criterion for correctness has not been that the system subdivide the input into the finest grain of subconstituents, but merely that all the subdivisions that the system proposes are in fact correct. Again, given a "gold standard" of analysis, we can use stricter evaluation criteria and distinguish between misplaced and omitted brackets, assuming that the program should produce a uniform level of linguistic analysis.

To get an idea of how this system works, consider consecutive and overlapping adjacent pairs of words in the input, and consider the vector of mutual information values produced by computing the mutual information values of each of these pairs. The initial assumption of this line of research was that a constituent boundary would be found at whatever location in this vector the mutual information reached a minimum. The idea is that it should be exactly at constituent boundaries at which, in general, word sequences are least correlated with each other. The initial hypothesis was that the smaller the mutual information, the more major the constituent boundary at that location. We call this approach to parsing *distituent* parsing,

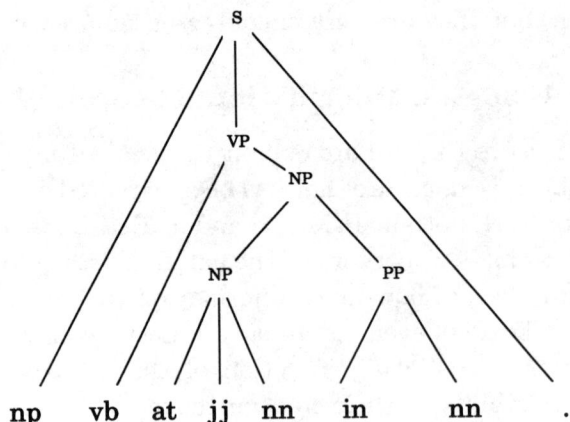

Figure 4:

An unlabeled bracketing determined by mutual information parsing.

because we are not looking for the *con*stituents, but rather for the breaks between them, which we call *dis*tituents.

As it turns out, this simple initial hypothesis doesn't work very well, in part because the context, single part of speech tags, is simply too small. However, the notion of mutual information can be extended from pairs of single tags to pairs of n-grams, i.e. pairs of n tag part-of-speech sequences. From this point of view, we can view an n-gram as a bigram of an n_1-gram and an immediately adjacent n_2-gram, where $n_1 + n_2 = n$. The mutual information of this bigram is

$$\mathcal{MI}(n_1\text{-gram}, n_2\text{-gram}) = \log \frac{\mathcal{P}[n\text{-gram}]}{\mathcal{P}[n_1\text{-gram}]\mathcal{P}[n_2\text{-gram}]}.$$

Notice that there are $(n-1)$ ways of partitioning an n-gram. Thus, for each n-gram, there is an $(n-1)$ vector of mutual information values. For a given n-gram $x_1 \ldots x_n$, we can define the mutual information values of x by:

$$\begin{aligned}\mathcal{MI}_n^k(x_1 \ldots x_n) &= \mathcal{MI}(x_1 \ldots x_k, x_{k+1} \ldots x_n) \\ &= \log \frac{\mathcal{P}(x_1 \ldots x_n)}{\mathcal{P}(x_1 \ldots x_k)\mathcal{P}(x_{k+1} \ldots x_n)}\end{aligned}$$

where $1 \leq k < n$.

Notice that, in the above equation, for each $\mathcal{MI}_n^k(x)$, the numerator, $\mathcal{P}(x_1 \ldots x_n)$, remains the same while the denominator, $\mathcal{P}(x_1 \ldots x_k)\mathcal{P}(x_{k+1} \ldots x_n)$, depends on k. Thus, the mutual information value achieves its minimum at the point where the denominator is maximized. The empirical claim tested by our work in parsing is that the minimum is achieved when the two components of this n-gram are in two different constituents, i.e. when $x_k x_{k+1}$ is a distituent. Our experiments show that this claim is largely true with a few interesting exceptions.

A straightforward approach would assign each potential distituent a single real number corresponding to the extent to which its context suggests it is a distituent. But the simple extension of bigram mutual information assigns each potential distituent a number for each n-gram of which it is a part. The question remains how to combine these numbers in order to achieve a valid measure of distituency.

Empirical studies show that a useful way to combine mutual information values is, for each possible distituent xy, to take a weighted sum of the mutual information values of all possible pairings of n-grams ending with x and n-grams beginning with y, within a fixed size window. So, for a window of size $w = 4$, given the context $x_1 x_2 x_3 x_4$, the generalized mutual information of $x_2 x_3$:

$$\mathcal{GMI}_4(x_1 x_2, x_3 x_4)$$
$$= k_1 \mathcal{MI}(x_2, x_3) + k_2 \mathcal{MI}(x_2, x_3 x_4) + k_3 \mathcal{MI}(x_1 x_2, x_3) + k_4 \mathcal{MI}(x_1 x_2, x_3 x_4)$$

which is equivalent to

$$\log\left(k \frac{\mathcal{P}[x_2 x_3]\mathcal{P}[x_2 x_3 x_4]\mathcal{P}[x_1 x_2 x_3]\mathcal{P}[x_1 x_2 x_3 x_4]}{[\mathcal{P}[x_2]\mathcal{P}[x_3]\mathcal{P}[x_1 x_2]\mathcal{P}[x_3 x_4]]^2}\right).$$

In general, the generalized mutual information of any given bigram xy in the context $x_1 \ldots x_{i-1} x y y_1 \ldots y_{j-1}$ is equivalent to

$$\log\left(\frac{\prod_{X \text{ crosses } xy} k_X \mathcal{P}[X]}{\prod_{X \text{ does not cross } xy} \mathcal{P}[X]^{(i+j)/2}}\right).$$

This equation shows that $\mathcal{GMI}$ is just the ratio of the probabilities of all the n-grams that cross the potential distituent boundary in question to all of the n-grams at the same scale that touch the boundary but do not cross it, which is intuitively just the kind of measure we want. Furthermore, this formula behaves in a manner consistent with one's expectation of a generalized mutual information statistic. It incorporates all of the mutual information data within the given window in a symmetric manner. Since it is the sum of bigram mutual information values, its behavior parallels that of bigram mutual information.

Our experiments have shown that minima in generalized mutual information values correlate well with breaks in syntactic structure, in general, and that more major constituent boundaries are reflected, in general, in lower relative minima in values of $\mathcal{GMI}$. However, there turn out to be a handful of important exceptions to the hypothesis that constituent boundaries are always reflected in lower $\mathcal{GMI}$ values. To combat this limited set of specific circumstances in which the hypothesis fails, we use a small (4 rule, 8 symbol) *distituent grammar*, which indicates when two parts of speech *cannot* remain in the same constituent. The details of how the parsing algorithm itself, and how this symbolic distituent grammar is combined with a largely statistical parsing process can be found in [16]. As stated above, this approach misplaces about 2-3 brackets per sentence of length less than 15, and about 5-6 brackets per sentence of length between 30 and 60.

5 Conclusion

The past five years have seen the beginning of a major shift of research focus in natural language processing. For twenty years, the center of the research effort was focused on systems which work well only in applications in which users can be depended upon to shift their usage to match the limitations of the system. We are now beginning to see the emergence of a new generation of systems that attempt to both extract information from and summarize pre-existing text from real-word domains. To achieve high coverage in such systems, a wide variety of research breakthroughs will be necessary. One such advance which is critical to truly wide-coverage systems is a technology which allows the automatic acquisition of linguistic structure through the analysis of both literal and annotated text corpora. Research results already in hand suggest that significant progress in this area, at least in the area of syntax, may occur in the next few years.

References

[1] Ballard, B. and Biermann A., 1979. "Programming in Natural Language: NLC as a prototype." *ACM National Conference*, Detroit, MI.

[2] Benello, J., Mackie A., Anderson J., 1989. "Syntactic Category Disambiguation with Neural Networks," *Computer Speech and Language*, Vol. 3, No. 3.

[3] Brill, E., D. Magerman, M. Marcus and B. Santorini 1990. "Deducing Linguistic Structure from the Statistics of Large Corpora," *Proceedings*

of the *DARPA Speech and Natural Language Workshop, June 1990,* Palo Alto: Morgan-Kaufman.

[4] Chomsky, N. 1957. *Syntactic Structures.* s'Gravenhage: Mouton.

[5] Chomsky, N. 1965. *Aspects of the Theory of Syntax.* Cambridge, MA: MIT Press.

[6] Church, K. 1988. "A Stochastic Parts Program and Noun Phrase Parser for Unrestricted Text," *Proceedings of the Second Conference on Applied Natural Language Processing.* Austin, Texas.

[7] Church, K. and Gale, W. 1990. "Enhanced Good-Turing and Cat-Cal: Two New Methods for Estimating Probabilities of English Bigrams." *Computers, Speech and Language.*

[8] Church, K. and Hanks, P. 1989. "Word Association Norms, Mutual Information, and Lexicography," *Proceedings of the 27th Annual Conference of the Association of Computational Linguistics.*

[9] Fano, R. 1961. *Transmission of Information.* New York: MIT Press.

[10] Francis, W. and Kučera, H. 1982. *Frequency Analysis of English Usage: Lexicon and Grammar.* Boston, Mass.: Houghton Mifflin Company.

[11] Harris, Z. S. 1951. *Structural Linguistics.* Chicago: University of Chicago Press.

[12] Harris, Z. S. 1968. *Mathematical Structures of Language.* New York: Wiley.

[13] Hindle, D. 1986. "Deterministic Parsing of Syntactic Non-fluencies," *Proceedings of the 21st Annual Conference of the Association for Computational Linguistics.*

[14] Hindle, D. 1989. "Acquiring Lexical Disambiguation Rules from Text," *Proceedings of the 27th Annual Conference of the Association for Computational Linguistics.*

[15] Jelinek, F. 1985. "Self-organizing Language Modeling for Speech Recognition." IBM Report.

[16] Magerman, D. and Marcus, M. 1990. "Parsing a Natural Language Using Mutual Information Statistics," *Proceedings of AAAI-90,* Boston, MA.

[17] Marcus, M. 1980. *A Theory of Syntactic Recognition for Natural Language.* Cambridge, MA: MIT Press.

[18] Nagao, M., J. Tsujii, and J. Nakamura. 1985. "The Japanese Government project for machine translation," in J. Slocum, ed., *Machine Translation Systems*, Cambridge: Cambridge University Press.

[19] Petrick, S. 1981. "Field-testing the transformational question answering (TQA) system," *Proceedings of the 19th Annual Conference of the Association for Computational Linguistics*.

[20] Quirk, R., S. Greenbaum, G. Leech, and J. Svartik. 1985. *A Comprehensive Grammar of the English Language*. London: Longman.

[21] Weischedel, R. et al. 1990. "Natural Language Processing", in *Annual Review of Computer Science*, 4:435-452.

[22] Winograd, T. 1972. *Understanding Natural Language*. New York: Academic Press.

Chapter 7
What Does Theoretical Physics Have to Say About Information Science?

P. W. Anderson[*]

1 Introduction

In the past decade there has grown up a remarkable synergy among a number of previously quite separate fields in physics, mathematics, biology, and computer science. Of course, it is healthy to examine skeptically the claims made by physicists to have "solved" this or that classic problem in someone else's field such as complex optimization, evolution theory, or brain theory, and very often the new point of view has indeed no immediate relevance to the questions the biologist or computer scientist wants answered. Such attitudes are familiar to theoretical physicists who are quite used to the fact that their statistical mechanical theory of ferromagnetism, for instance, will never help pin notes on your refrigerator or predict a good chemical composition for a permanent magnet. Nonetheless it should be the nature of science to welcome understanding wherever it may come from, even if it isn't invented here and doesn't solve the problems you already know are problems, but only seems to pose annoying new ones. I'm trying to say that I recognize that the arrogance of theoretical physicists can be a real cross to bear but sometimes theory can lead to very exciting insights.

A good way to begin a summary of these developments is with the historical context. From the physics side, this dates from the first realizations, by Hammersley and then by myself, that the statistical physics of what we now call quenched random systems contains fundamentally new behaviors and is, in fact, new physics. Quenched random systems are those which can be treated in the "thermodynamic limit" $N \to \infty$ in that they contain a very large number of separate simple elements, but in which those elements are randomly connected in some fixed or "quenched" manner. In physics itself such phenomena as percolation due to random connections, localization due to random scattering, and gellation due to random cross-linking arise from

---
[*]Joseph Henry Laboratories of Physics, Jadwin Hall, Princeton University, Princeton, NJ 08544.

such systems—phenomena which in each case consist in the possibility of some kind of "freezing" transition at which motion stops. While all of these examples may in fact be of interest, as models for other sciences, the one which has turned out to be most useful is the "spin glass model", which appeared about 1975. In this kind of model, N identical units, which are called "spins", S_i, are coupled by interactions J_{ij} which are chosen randomly and independently from a distribution which, to be interesting, must contain both signs of J. In the simplest "Ising" version, S_i is an "Ising" spin which may take on the discrete values ± 1, and the physics is controlled by an energy function

$$\mathcal{H} = \sum J_{ij} S_i S_j$$

for which one optimizes the free energy

$$F = -T \ln \sum_{S_i = \pm 1} \cdots \sum_{S_N = \pm 1} \exp[-\frac{1}{T} J_{ij} S_i S_j].$$

At $T = 0$, F is then the minimum value of the energy $\mathcal{H}$. Many generalizations are possible, as e.g., to continuous, dynamical, or quantum spins, etc.

In the early work (1975–79) on this model (see [1] for an excellent review and compilation of reprints in the field, and [2,3,4,5,6]) it was shown *(a)* that it is susceptible to analysis by statistical mechanics, and has, in general, a phase transition at a certain temperature T_{SG} below which the spins "freeze" into some specific average relative configuration; *(b)* that in order to solve it, not only a new technology must be invented (the "replica" method or the "cavity" technique of TAP as reinterpreted by Virasoro [7]) but a new statistical mechanics of non-unique outcomes must be invented [3,6].

Both (a) and (b) are very important results for the applications which later ensued. (a) tells us that all the powerful conceptual structure of statistical mechanics is available to us, notably the property of "self-averaging"— every part of a large system is like every other part, that is, in some real sense—and the ideas of extensive (of order N) variables such as entropy, energy, and intensive "force" variables of order unity such as temperature. There can be phase transitions, at which the distribution of states of a given energy is singular at a given (intensive) T_c and thus extensive (of order N) E_c. (b) tells us, however, that we get new and interesting properties compared to ordinary phase transitions like melting or ferromagnetism, and, for instance, it tells us that true ergodicity is missing: configurations group into non-communicating sets. This is the only possible interpretation of the existence of an entropy of order N which is singular at a given T_c and E_c. All of these ideas depend on the model being at least a limiting case of a real statistical mechanics problem, with a large number of similar entities having some locality property.

THEORETICAL PHYSICS/INFORMATIONAL SCIENCE

2 Optimization and Complexity

It is time we made the connection to the other sciences and, particularly, to computer science. This was begun by Scott Kirkpatrick[4] who noticed that finding the ground state of the spin glass Hamiltonian is equivalent to a well-known example of an "NP-complete" complex optimization problem (I believe the particular problem is called, for some reason, the "matching problem"). NP completeness is a category of problems which cannot be solved in polynomial time. We, on the one hand, had found what we called "the solution" of the spin glass for large N; but computer scientists were telling us we could not do so in a time of less than order $\exp(N^2)$. This apparent paradox is of course not one at all, and, in fact, we had already noticed this as a difficulty: to find the *actual* ground state of a large simulated spin glass seemed to be extremely slow and difficult, even though we would usually find that after some time we came to nearly exactly the right energy to order N. The NP complete problem however, is to find the *exact* lowest energy, and *and the state which goes with it*, whereas our solution only predicts the energy and leaves the state that gives that energy unknown. It also only finds the energy to order N, with terms of order unity left unknown. Nonetheless, we had actually learned a lot about at least one NP-complete problem: enough, for instance to understand why, in this case, it was not possible to find an algorithm for the lowest energy: namely that there are many solutions with energies that are "good enough"—to order N—and that each of these many solutions is a strong attractor for any optimization procedure which allows only finitely many changes in spins: but only one of these is the right one! These ideas[1] were discussed by Stein, Palmer and myself[2] as well as Kirkpatrick and Toulouse [9]. The picture is of a large number of deep "basins of attraction," "valleys" with low values of the energy

$$\sum J_{ij} S_i S_j$$

as a function of the vector of configurations

$$\vec{x} = \{S_i\} \ .$$

These basins must be separate up to energies of the order E_c with

$$(E_c - E_0) \propto N \ ,$$

except possibly for a set of "passes" which are so narrow or convoluted that they contribute nothing to the entropy

$$S(E_c) = \frac{1}{N} \ln \left(\# \ of \ configs. \ of \ energy \ \leq E_c \right)$$

---

[1] The first paper foreshadowing this is a little-known one [8].
[2] These discussions were the basis of a number of further developments, but no one reprint covers them.

and are therefore exponentially hard to find. These early intuitions have been very much refined in the work of Miguel Virasoro of a few years ago [7], but what they amount to is a realization of the simple but profound consequences of phase transitions, which must always signal some kind of non-ergodic behavior.

Just to demonstrate the method, a couple of my students (Fu and Liao) [10,11] used it to estimate the limiting cost in the graph bipartition problem, a problem which turned out to resemble, but to be trickier than, the matching problem.

Kirkpatrick and Gelatt [12] in one of the most fruitful applications of these ideas, based an algorithm for complex optimization problems on these ideas in the form of the now well-known "simulated annealing" procedure. The principle behind this method is to convert the optimization problem of your choice into a statistical mechanics problem and introduce a "temperature". Then, using well-known algorithms for simulating statistical mechanics, one starts at a high "temperature" above the inevitable freezing point and "anneals" the temperature in a programmed way to $T = 0$, where hopefully one has a very low value of the cost function.

There is much that still needs to be understood about these statistical methods for optimization problems. The computer mathematicians' theorems and the statistical mechanical theorems have a fascinating way of resembling each other but not meshing. The existence of replica symmetry breaking, which is the jargon term for having many well-separated deep minima, always seems to signal NP completeness but by no means vice versa. Most often, the problem lies in the rather ill-defined question of measure in the space of problems. The statistical mechanics theory can only operate by averaging over problems, in a sense—averaging over some distribution of J_{ij}'s, hence picking a definite kind of measure in problem space. This measure may have little to do with what the computer person may consider a sensible or typical problem, and certainly NP completeness, for instance, has no reference to an "average" or typical problem.

One interesting development which might throw some light on these questions has happened in neural networks theory. Elizabeth Gardner[3] whose work I will mention later, has recently shown how to study a kind of *inverse* problem: to ask how big is the space of *problem* $\{J_{ij}\}$ for which a given configuration $S_1, S_2 \ldots S_N$ is the *solution*? This almost seems more to resemble certain of the computer science questions more than the *direct* spin-glass problem. But this is strictly speculative territory.

---

[3]Dr. Gardner's work is well represented in a memorial volume [13].

3   Collective Computation

There are two more—at least—interesting applications of this kind of physical theory outside its origins in materials science. Already in 1973 [14] with antecedents long before in the work of Marr [15] Leon Cooper had called attention to the possibilities inherent in what he called "collective computation", as a model for brain function: Marr, particularly, had emphasized the enormously redundant connectivity of actual brain anatomy, and Hebb as well as Marr suggested that modifiable synapses might be the vital elements of brain function (synapses are the "excitatory" or "inhibiting" connections between neurons).

The first few attempts to realize schemes for collective computation were discouraged by the AI community or otherwise unsuccessful. Finally, however, two more or less viable approaches simultaneously appeared on the scene, at first appearing quite different: the multilayer perceptron with back propagation [16] and the Hopfield spin glass analog [17]. Apparently utterly dissimilar, the differences now appear to be evaporating.

Both view a neuron as a much over-simplified object which simply sums its inputs, with a threshold, in order to decide whether or not to produce output. Thus the neuron is a generalized spin S_i with value $S_i = \pm 1$, which can send signals to other neurons j, which then respond according to the sign of the sum

$$\text{(1)} \qquad h_j = \sum_i S_i J_{ij}$$

$$\text{(2)} \qquad S_j = sgn(h_j)$$

depending on the strengths of the synapses J_{ij} from i to j. As Hopfield proposed in 1982, we could therefore think of what is going on as an algorithm for minimizing with respect to S_j

$$\sum_i S_i J_{ij} S_j$$

and if $J_{ij} = J_{ij}$ this minimizes the double sum

$$\sum_{ij} S_i J_{ij} S_j$$

and hence leads to a unique outcome for the whole system. We can also introduce a temperature, which allows the system to make a few errors, with $S_i = \tanh \beta h_i/2$ instead of $sgn\, h_i$. Hopfield's is not the only choice of J_{ij} which leads to a unique outcome. One particularly important one is the tridiagonal J_{ij} matrix with $J_{ij} = 0\ i > j$, so that there is a hierarchy of neurons, with earlier ones influencing later ones but not vice versa. This is a generalized version of the "multilayer perceptron" of Rumelhart and others, which has often been seen as completely different from the Hopfield scheme. Although there is no Hamiltonian to be optimized, this, like the symmetric case, has only "point attractors" in its dynamics. It seems that, in fact, a very large class of J_{ij} choices have this uniqueness property—again, this is one of the results of Miss Gardner's very important work of the years 1987–89 [13].

In her work, she started from the above equation linking S_i and $h_i = \sum_j J_{ij} S_j$ and instead of treating the configuration S_i as the unknown, she supposes that an a priori given set of configurations $x^\alpha = \{S_i^\alpha\}$ are to be attractors of this procedure considered as a dynamical process. This then is treated as a statistical mechanical problem determining the J_{ij} or at least the entropy of the distribution of J_{ij}'s which can satisfy all the x^α's. In general, her J_{ij}'s are not symmetrical or tridiagonal, yet all of them have unique point attractors. They tend to resemble perceptrons rather more than Hopfield nets but to be neither.

If we equip either scheme with modifiable synapses, they seem to be able to learn a great deal of information as a context-addressible memory or to learn to do various tasks such as pattern recognition. The perceptron has been the more thoroughly tested as a practical device, but both schemes, or in fact the possibility of general J_{ij}, has been extensively analysed mathematically, in the sense of studying how big is the memory capacity for a given case, how robust the memories are, etc. Especially Sompolinsky [18] and Marc Mézard and his group [19] have achieved a great many interesting results.

Aside from these rather esoteric considerations, are neural nets making any contact with reality? The most serious uses have been in the form of perceptron learning machines, which in the hands of Sejnowski and others do seem to work. I am not really competent to review questions of hardware realization—there are others here who are much more qualified. As for whether the brain works this way, there is the serious problem that the models for neurons and synapses are schematic in the extreme, and undoubtedly real brains do things differently and probably better; neural nets are merely, in this case, a demonstration of possibility; which, however, is very important indeed.

4 Evolution

The final area which has been influenced by the spin-glass type of development is the general theory of evolution. Stein and I, in 1980 [20], had already conceived the idea of looking at the genetic code as a string of spin-variables undergoing dynamical time development in the course of reproduction. Influenced by Hopfield's borrowing of spin glass ideas for neural nets, I realized in 1981–82 that random interactions could be used to model a "fitness landscape" for "organisms" conceived of in this way, as strings of genetic information.

Our particular interest was in modeling the prebiotic origin of life, using a mechanism envisaged by H. Kuhn [21], RNA replication and autocatalysis driven by temperature cycling. A population of "organisms" (strings of ± spins S_i) is encouraged to conjugate randomly in pairs during a "cool" cycle, and if two shorter strings (RNA polymers) are conjugated end to end on a third, longer one, they are allowed to bond to each other giving a longer single RNA polymer. The strings are then subjected to a "heating" cycle where they separate and also encounter a "fitness function" which in our work is a spin-glass Hamiltonian, and which serves as a criterion for survival into the next conjugation. Thus our "fitness landscape" is a spin glass function. The concept of a random *rugged fitness landscape* has caught on with a number of workers, such as Gérard Weisbuch, Peter Schuster and his collaborator Walter Fontana, and especially Stuart Kauffman [22]. (Some early aspects of these ideas were put forward by M. Eigen and his collaborators [23].) It is not confined to the Eigen-Kuhn "RNA only" scenario; Kauffman points out that the random-fitness can simply result from random catalytic activity for a given arbitrary reaction $A + B \to C$ of either complex peptide chains or RNA molecules or both. In all versions, however, the general scheme is that of what Stu Kauffman calls "hill-climbing in a rugged landscape": the populations seek out the local maxima of fitness. If the landscape is of the spin glass type, there will be many such local maxima, and populations can easily be trapped in relatively unfavorable ones, from which they may or may not be rescued by rare events involving members of the population which have strayed rather far from the local optimum. Another important feature of this scenario is variety: we can have populations in many different minima. Whether or not this scenario can give us a satisfactory account of the origin of life, it certainly is a fascinating and suggestive model for the way biological evolution takes place. Kauffman in particular, has made extensive computer studies of the kinetics of random hill-climbing, showing, for instance, how increasing complexity can pay off better than trying to continually improve at the same level of complexity. Recently he has also made some studies of co-evolution models as a way of providing computer models for ecological phenomena. Kauffman favors a generalization of the original spin glass interactions which he calls the "n-k" model; this can be shown to be equivalent to a multi-spin spin glass interaction and the differences from general spin-glass interactions are not really very important relatively.

What connection is there with reality? Very little indeed, except perhaps with the fascinating experiments on very primitive RNA organisms by Eigen and his collaborators, demonstrating the genuine existence of fitness optima and fluctuations around them: his idea of quasispecies. I again see the whole scheme in terms of the very important, more or less philosophical, problem of *possibility*: can one imagine a scheme which genuinely does evolve new organisms, of increasing complexity with time, with statistical properties which resemble the actual course of evolution? Can one get hold of at least some hints as to the requisite rates of evolution and of complexification, etc? Most of the more quantitative approach remains to be done—but at least one can begin to do it.

In both of these last two areas there is a high methodological and philosophical barrier to progress. The theorist feels that one can go on forever gathering more or less "anecdotal" empirical evidence on evolution or brain function without any hope of genuine progress unless there is some theoretical framework to build upon. The empiricist, on the other hand, can see little resemblance between the real object and the theoretical framework, and questions its value. For the time being, we shall just have to accept these facts, and do our best to tolerate different points of view.

References

[1] M. Mézard, G. Parisi, and M. A. Virasoro, eds, *Spin Glass Theory and Beyond*, World Scientific, Teaneck, N.J., (1987).

[2] S.F. Edwards and P.W. Anderson, *J. Phys.* **F5**, p.965 (1975).

[3] G. Toulouse, *Comm. Phys.* **2**, p.115 (1977).

[4] S. Kirkpatrick and D. Sherrington, *Phys. Rev.* **B 17**, p.4384 (1978).

[5] J. R. L. de Almeida and D. J. Thouless, *J. Phys.* **A11**, p.983 (1978).

[6] G. Parisi, *Physics Letters* **73A**, p.203 (1979).

[7] M. Mézard, C. Parisi and M. A. Virasoro, *Europhysics Lett.* **1**, p.77 (1986).

[8] A. J. Bray and M. A. Moore, *J. Phys. C* **13**, p.469 (1980).

[9] S. Kirkpatrick and G. Toulouse, *J. Physique*, **46**, p.1277 (1985).

[10] Y. Fu and P. W. Anderson, *J. Phys.* **A**, p.1605 (1986).

[11] Wuwell Liao, *Phys. Rev. Lett* **12**, p.1625 (1987).

[12] S. Kirkpatrick, C.D. Gelatt Jr., M.P. Vecchi, *Science* **220**, p.4598 (1983).

[13] *Journal of Physics* **A22**, #12 (1989) & *Journal of Physics* **A21**, p.257 (1988).

[14] L. N. Cooper, in *Collective Properties of Physical Systems*, ed. Lundquist and Lundquist, Nobel Foundation, Stockholm, (1973).

[15] D. Marr, *Vision*, Freeman (1982).

[16] D. E. Rumelhart, G. F. Hinton, R. J. Williams, *Nature*, **323**, p.533 (1986).

[17] J. J. Hopfield, *PNAS*, **79**, p.2554, (1982).

[18] D. J. Amit, H. Gutfreund, H. Sompolinsky, *Phys. Rev.*, **A32**, p.1007 (1985).

[19] M. Mézard, J. P. Nadal, G. Toulouse, *J. Physique* **47**, p.1457 (1986).

[20] D. Rokshar, D. L. Stein and P. W. Anderson, *J. Mol Evolution* **233**, p.119 (1986).

[21] H. Kuhn, *Orig. Life* **9**, p.137 (1978).

[22] S. Kauffman, forthcoming book, Oxford U. Press (1990).

[23] M. Eigen, in *Disordered Systems and Biological Organization*, Bienenstock, Fogeler and Weisbuch eds, Springer, Berlin (1985) p.25; Also, see M. Eigen and R. Winkler-Ostatitsch, The Game of Life (paperback).

Panel Session

Chairman:
Professor Amari
University of Tokyo

Panelists

Philip Anderson, Princeton University
Walter Freeman, University of California at Berkeley
C. W. Gear, NEC Research Institute
H. T. Kung, Carnegie Mellon University
Mitchell Marcus, University of Pennsylvania
Robert Tarjan, Princeton University and NEC Research Institute
Leslie Valiant, Harvard University and NEC Research Institute

October 29, 1990

Abstract

The final part of the conference was a panel discussion with audience participation. Two topics were considered, each for one hour. Each topic was introduced by one panelist, a second panelist responded, and then the topic was discussed by other panel members and the audience. The written form was transcribed from tapes of the session. Each speaker had the opportunity to propose changes to the written form (but was requested not to do change the content in any significant way). The final revisions were made by the editor who accepts responsibility for the errors and apologizes to the panelists if he misrepresented their views.

1 Topic 1: Relationships between Computers and the Brain

Introduction   Professor Amari
Response   Professor Freeman

Amari

I would like to start the discussion on the modern computer and the brain. How are those two alike and how are they not alike? After my short presentation, Professor Walter Freeman will "attack" my point of view and provide further material for discussion.

We are very much interested in similarities and intrinsic differences between computers and brains. We believe they are very different in their fundamental information processing styles, so I begin with a very intuitive view of the thinking process in the human brain.

There seem to be two different types of thinking processes. One uses symbols to represent information. Information is summarized in concepts, which are a very concentrated, symbolic representation of information. Logical combinations of such symbols are the origin of logic. Logical inference can be performed using symbols. This type of symbolic processing is sequential in nature, and if we know the routine of a particular symbolic process, we can implement it in the form of a computer program.

We say that symbolic processing is a higher-order intellectual method of thinking because only human beings can think in this manner; monkeys do not think in this manner.

However, we know that this is not the only style of thinking in our brain. We think of some things intuitively; we cannot explain why such certain ideas come into our mind, but, by unifying many types of information, we sometimes suddenly find very good ideas. There must be some information processing taking place in our brain, but in this case, everything proceeds in the subconsciousness, and information is represented by a pattern of excitation in the brain. Parallel dynamics occur by the mutual interaction of active elements (neurons). As a result of the dynamics, suddenly a good idea emerges. Learning is very important to modify or improve this type of thinking. We have well-known mathematical theorems on the principles of the first style of information processing: there are mathematical theories devoted to logic and symbols. They are for example, Turin computability theory, mathematical logic, etc. Moreover, we have the technology to realize such types of information processing. This has lead to the modern computer and we understand these computers very well. On the other hand, we do not know much about brains, but we believe that people can function very well using the intuitive style of information processing and that combination of the two completely different types of information processing produces very intellectual and efficient thinking methods.

It is very difficult to establish a mathematical foundation for the intuitive, parallel style of information processing. If one could find the principles underlying this type of information processing, it might be possible to construct neural computers. If we could unify these two different types of computers, we would have a better understanding of both.

I have talked about two different types of information processing, sequential and parallel. We know much about the sequential type; we want to understand the information principle underlying parallel information processing, distributed information representation, and learnability. If we are able to find this information principle, we can realize it in hardware to produce neural computers.

In order to make neural computers, it is necessary to study our own brain. Should we imitate the structure of the real brain as faithfully as possible? I don't think so. It's not wise to imitate the actual brain. We should realize the information principles used in the brain in a completely different way using modern technology.

However, to understand the information principles, it is useful to study the brain. From the information principle point of view, our brain is merely one example, one realization of this type of information principle. We may call it the biological realization, because the brain realizes this type of information principle by the process of a long history of evolution and use of biological material. The brain couldn't use silicon technology or something like that, instead it uses biological molecules or molecular devices. So the engineering realization takes a very different form.

It is suggestive to compare the relation between brains and computers with that between birds and airplanes. Some AI people use this analogy to say that research on neural computers is nonsense. They say that birds and planes are completely different. Planes should never try to fly like a bird; they would crash, causing a disaster. Therefore, neither should one imitate the brain to make neural computers.

However, there is a common fundamental principle underlying the two types of flying objects, it is the principle of fluid dynamics described by the Navier Stokes equation. It elucidates the mutual interaction of a solid body and a fluid, their force exchange, disturbances on the flow, etc. The bird has evolved, by using biological materials, soft wings and some muscles and so on, to realize the flying function to fit well with the fundamental principle of fluid dynamics.

On the other hand, the human engineer studied this principle and invented a different realization of the same principle using solid materials. So the artificial flying objects are very different from birds in their materials and architectures, but they are based on the same fundamental principle. I believe that the same holds between the brain and future computers.

I have said that there are two different types of information principle; one is serial and the other is parallel. We should understand and realize both of the two different principles. We have already realized the first. The problem is how to understand the second information principle based on parallel, distributed processing having learnability.

There are of course, many methods of approach. There are, for example, the biological approach, the application-oriented approach, the hardware device approach, and the theoretical approach. Current research on neural networks is very active and fashionable. However, in order to have a true development, a solid mathematical basis is necessary. Mathematical theories should explain what is the capability of information processing using nonlinear, mutually interacting elements and what is its limitation as an information processing system. Abstract mathematical models are useful in order to understand this type of information principle. Of course, a mathematical model of the actual brain might be very important, too. However, it is easier first to build an abstract mathematical model to explain the information principle underlying the use of parallel, distributed, learnable systems, and then to apply this to the elucidation of the actual brain. This is because the brain is just one realization of this principle.

By using a very simple model, we can analyze it mathematically, point out its capabilities and its limitations. From the theoretical point of view, the limitations are much more important than the capabilities. For example, we can study a neural network of a simple architecture to point out the fundamental characteristics of its dynamics: which type of dynamics can be implemented in such an architecture and which type cannot. Then we can study a more complex architecture to realize other dynamical behaviors, and so on.

I would like to indicate a new direction for future research on neural networks. It is based on *information geometry*.

Consider the set of all the neural networks of a fixed architecture. One network is specified by a set of synaptic coefficients w_{ij} of connections. Its input-output relation can be written in terms of connection weights. We usually take one neural network and study the property of that network by computer simulation. However, I propose to adopt a wider point of view.

Consider the sets of all the transformations from input signal space X to the output signal space Z (this is a function space, of course, of infinite dimensions). The set M of transformations which a given type of neural networks can realize is a submanifold embedded in the function space of all the transformations. The dimensionality of this neural net manifold M is, of course, finite. It depends on the number of synapses, n^2, or something similar, where n is the number of neurons. Then, an interesting problem is to know in what shape this neural network manifold M takes in the entire function space. We need to approximate a general transformation, f in S by a neural network in M. What is the best way to find the best neural network which approximates this one? Can we find the best one by learning? By learning dynamics, starting from an initial state, the neural network moves in M to find the optimal dynamics in M. What are the properties of such dynamics in M? We can think about the capacity of neural networks in the submanifold M in comparison to the function space of the transformations. Also we need to study what type of approximation is better, and what is the appropriate distance between two transformations (or neural networks).

If the function space S is Euclidean, that is, L_2 space, everything is very easy to understand. However we have some good reason to believe that it is not Euclidean. It is a Riemannian manifold equipped with a pair of dual affine connections. We need to construct an information geometry on the manifold of all the transformations and the neural network manifold. The Riemannian mapping in the neural manifold tells us how different two neural networks are. Unfortunately I have no time to talk about information geometry[1] which has been established with the help of probability theory and statistics.

In conclusion, I would like to point out that we need a number of new methods of approach to neural dynamics, which is a very complex nonlinear system. Statistical neural dynamics is one approach, and the algorithmic computational theory provides another. However, I would like to emphasize that information geometry is very important for examining the capabilities of neural networks from a global point of view.

I talked from a purely mathematical or information theoretical point of view, so now is the time for a biologist, Professor Freeman, to attack this naive and simple point of view.

Freeman

Thank you very much Professor Amari. You embarrass me with the richness of your display of the possibilities inherent in the applications of new forms of geometry to the understanding of the immensely complex problems that we face in information management with computers.

To talk about the difference between the computers and the brain is like beating a dead horse, and I might say, incidentally if I could put a little error correction in my speech, that my only point of disagreement with Professor Amari might have arisen from his original title, "Computers and the Mind." He skillfully avoided this by changing course in mid stream; that was his error correction! In any case there is a well known book written by John von Neuman, published posthumously by his widow, "The Computer and the Brain[2]", in which he laid out the fundamental differences between brains and computers as long ago as 1958.

It is a poignant book, because it is a confession of a disappointed seeker who had hoped to invent the calculus which would essentially pave the way toward artificial intelligence in a true form. He came to realize that, in fact, there are major differences between his machines, von Neuman machines

---

[1] See, for example, S. Amari, *Differential Methods in Statistics*, Springer Lecture Notes in Statistics, **28**, 1985, S. Amari, Differential Geometry of a parametric family of invertible linear systems – Riemannian metric, dual affine connections and divergence, *Mathematical Systems Theory*, **20**, pp 53-82, 1987, and S. Amari & T. S. Han, Statistical inference under multi-terminal rate restrictions – a differential geometrical approach, *IEEE Trans. Information Theory*, **IT-35**, pp 217-227, 1989.

[2] Yale University Press, New Haven, 1958.

as we think of them now, and the brain. These differences are: arithmetic versus logical depth; analog versus digital; serial versus parallel; and so on. Basically, he came down to the conclusion that, whatever the language of the brain is, it is not mathematics, or at least what we consciously and explicitly consider to be mathematics.

Certainly we can describe brain functions with mathematical operations, but can it really be said that the brain is using mathematics? That's something that needs to be resolved. In any case the point that I've been struck by in coming here, looking back on this perspective of the last 40 years of development of our machines and their relations to our brains, is highlighted in the phrase that was put forward for us yesterday in the ceremony for dedication of the NEC Research Institute facility: "C&C", which, it was explained, meant variously "communication and computers", or "computers and cognition."

You recall that when this phrase was introduced 40 years ago by Norbert Wiener in his book, "Cybernetics", it was used to mean "Communication and Control" in man and machine. I think it is very significant that this word "control" has been dropped from "C&C". The military, of course, still have this in terms of their "Communication, Command and Control", but now it means "computers and cognition." I think there is implicit in this statement the meaning "computers and *cooperation*", and that it reflects a fundamental cultural change. It constitutes backing off from the notion of forward transmission of information for manipulation and for the seeing to it that our devices do what we want them to do, that they are nothing more than servo-mechanisms, our slaves. Now we have the idea emerging of a cooperative exchange of information for the furtherance of the good of everybody, for the induction of collaboration among multiple semi-autonomous units. This occurs not only among individuals in a civilized society, as we see now in Eastern Europe, and between nations as we see between our own country and Japan, but also now in our machines. And further there is a language by which we described this kind of cooperative process. It is the language of nonlinear dynamics. The phenomenon of emergent order, of self organization, in which large assemblies of semi-autonomous elements, any number you choose, by virtue of their weak interactions but on a global scale, give rise to large patterns which couldn't pre-exist without the interactions.

The next point I want to make is that serial computers process information, and that brains process meanings. Brains extract meaning by using interactions among nerve cells to form cooperative assemblies. It is now clear that chaotic dynamics creates information in the process of generating meaning. Forty years ago we were indebted to Shannon and Weaver for developing information theory for communications but they did this at an enormous price, which was to divorce information from meaning.

The result now is that we are being drowned, as Goodman said yesterday, in immense quantities of information over which we have no control. What we really want to know is: What does it mean? I submit that there is the inherent possibility in new cooperative machines to build them so that, just as I showed yesterday in the biological system, the first stage serves to reduce these immense quantities of information to manageable proportions and to extract their meanings. If that didn't happen right at the first stage of our visual, auditory, and olefactory systems, our brain would be incapacitated. I think in the future we look forward to the possibilities, and this is inherent in Professor Amari's description of neuronal information geometries, that the emergence of these global patterns of meaning from large masses of information will be facilitated by our cooperative computers acting like midwives, and that we will be far better in management and prediction of the cooperative processes which form our societies.

Comments from panel members and audience

Gear

I would like to return to the question of the computer and the mind. The January 1990 *Scientific American* contained two articles claiming to debate artificial intelligence. I believe the articles address two quite different questions: The Churchlands ask the question "Can a machine think?" This is a rather different issue to the one John Searle asks: "Is the brain's mind a computer program?" (He answers "No.") A computer program is only the passive part, there is an active part, the memory which is changing during execution, so the appropriate question, I believe, would be "Is the brain's mind executing a computer program?"

The Churchlands suggest that neural network computers may do something that symbolic, programmed computers can't do. I think there is only one sense in which they may, and that is simply speed. I claim that the two types of computers are equivalent in one sense: it is possible to simulate one on the other. We know it is possible to simulate a digital computer, in fact that's what we do when we build it out of various pieces of hardware and we simulate all the required logical operations. It is equally possible to simulate any sort of mathematically defined neural network on a digital computer. The only real difference is speed, and I think the question of speed raises two issues: the practical one is simply that we are interested in doing real problems with economic impact by the fastest or least expensive method, so it is possible that neural networks are good for some sorts of problems and digital computers are not. But when we come to the question of thinking, the speed issue raises the question: "Is there something essential in speed for thinking?" In other words if we produce an artifice that did the same operations as occur in our brains, but at a much slower pace, would we call it thinking?

I think this may have something to do with whether or not we believe a computer can think.

Mitchell Marcus

To raise another issue, I think that we also need to take into account the tension between cognitive models which are inherently continuous and the evidence from many cognitive domains that some key cognitive processes are both extremely symbolic and extremely formal. While there are real limits on what we know about the encoding of linguistic knowledge in our minds, there is very compelling evidence that both syntactic and phonological phenomena are fundamentally symbolic and not continuous. Not that I don't believe that some quasi-continuous processes aren't in operation. It just seems to me that we're only seeing one piece of the puzzle if we just look at phenomena which can be modelled easily by continuous methods. I deeply believe that a correct model of mind will look like the wave particle duality in some funny sense or other. I think that such a representation will cause the current signal-symbol barrier to appear as an artifact of the representation. Unfortunately, I have no good ideas about what this representation should look like. I'm concerned that we may lose sight of the fact that while our study of physiology may imply that the brain is a continuous device, that many cognitive systems appear to be symbolic and formal.

Amari

It's very interesting to discuss the duality between concentrated symbolism and distributed information representation.

Richard Linke (NEC Research Institute)

I would like to go back to Bill Gear's question: if we build a thinking machine but it thinks very slowly, are we satisfied to call it a thinking machine? The other side of the same coin is that there are machines such as the current chess playing machines which no one would call thinking machines but, nevertheless, appear to be close to the capability of beating most humans. At what point are we going to be willing to call this thinking? If, ultimately, those machines can, just by brute force and speed, solve any problem one can think of, will we call that thinking?

Anderson

I want to reinforce what Richard Linke just said. The brain, the human brain at least, seems to be the only object which does both in a sense, has both the parallel processing capability and the symbolic capability. Something perhaps really almost discontinuous happens when you combine a more or less linear thinking machine (a symbolic thinking machine that is a focus machine thinking about only one thing at a time, but is thinking very fast) with a set of perceptive techniques that necessarily have to be run in parallel. To what extent the thinking part of it also runs in parallel we do not know.

Somehow we use the parallel processing perceptual part to produce schemas to simplify the structure of the information. Then also we think about the structure in a sequential way and perhaps that is the nature of what we, out at the Santa Fe Institute, often call the C-Word: Consciousness. Possibly all this is true of lower animals too. I'm not one who believes that there are no animals that think or that operate in much the same way. I think in some cases the differences are less than the similarities.

Freeman

As a biologist, let me introduce the notion that even though our variables in the dynamics are continuous functions in time, because there exist continued aperiodic state transitions, the brain goes from one stage to the next in a discontinuous manner. The evolution of what an animal brain is generating in fact resembles more closely a set of frames in a motion picture, than it does a continuous trajectory. So these successive frames of meaning would serve as your candidates for these symbols.

So I have no problem with your introduction, let's say, of symbols into the biological computer.

Andrew T. Ogielski (Bellcore)

It struck me that, for a discussion about "neural computers," very little has been said about biological constraints on the structure of real brains and the architectural clues one might therefore obtain. First, there are power dissipation problems: making digital brains would cost a lot of power. Second there are connectivity constraints. We are only getting to this point in computing. And last but not least, I would like to see more emphasis on timing, but from another point of view: Neurons are rather slow, so it's marvelous that brains can work as fast as they do. I'm afraid I didn't quite understand Gear's remark about speed and thinking machines – today's devices are orders of magnitude faster than neurons, and the problem is that we do not yet know how to design brain-like circuits.

Gear

It's true that digital devices are orders of magnitude faster, but when we use them to simulate even relatively simple models, of, say, neurons, especially if we simulate them at the analog level with differential equations, they are no longer orders of magnitude faster, they are usually slower.

Ogielski

Yes that's what I meant: perhaps digital simulation is not the right way to go.

Gear

I was not suggesting that is the way to go, I am just claiming that there is an equivalence in the sense that one system can do what the other system can do and vice versa. The Churchland's, in their article for example, make the statement that neural networks will somehow allow computers to think whereas a conventional Turin model machine will not, and I can't accept that.

Eric Baum (NEC Research Institute)

I have a few comments on several of the preceding comments. First of all to Richard Linke's comment on computer chess: I don't think it's fair to say that the poor human is suffering under from lack of thinking power; most reasonable estimates would place the human brain substantially ahead of any current computer in its thinking power, and in fact a pessimist would argue that we will always have problems trying to duplicate the brain because it has so much more hardware than we can build in a computer. I don't think that's true either, but when a computer beats a human at chess, I would call it thinking. It's using a very different algorithm from the human, perhaps, but that's not a fair reason to say that it isn't thinking, and in fact if you let that computer think for month on how to move and it then was then able to beat Kasparov, I would say that, even though it was slow, that it was thinking and was doing an interesting thing. (That experiment might actually be interesting because I don't know if it's been done and the computer might very well beat Kasparov.)

Tarjan

Let me just respond to that. Actually, computers do much better at speed chess than at slow chess. If you give both the human and the computer more time, the human will slaughter the computer. If you speed up things sufficiently then anybody, even Kasparov, will lose to a computer.

Baum

I want to comment on Bill Gear's comment about neural networks. Les Valiant said yesterday that he viewed neural networks as an aspect of experimental learning, and I tend to agree with that. I think that most of the neural network community is not wedded to the fact that it's a biological model, and none of them are wedded to using threshold units. One of the main things that the neural network community has introduced is the notion of training. For the first 20 or 30 years of AI most everything was constructed by hand. One runs into the problem that one can't get beyond limited domains. An enormous amount of data is needed to deal with the world, and especially one needs incredibly intricate relationships between data items, so many that they can't really be computed by hand. This morning we heard Mitchell Marcus tell us that researchers are starting to use more and more learning in natural language research; I think that the future is with natural learning. With learning, the question is: will we be able to come up with good learning algorithms and develop machines that can emulate some aspects of humans.

Evolution has produced our brain over several billion years, with a certain amount of parallelism, but I expect with a lack of efficiency in its algorithm. We now have this marvelous brain plus some electronic hardware that we are able to build. We would like to produce in a relatively short period of time better algorithms for performing all the things done by our brain. So a question which arises is to estimate our relative efficiency at computing versus the efficiency of evolution. I wonder if anybody has any way of estimating that?

Gear

I would like to comment that there is a stability that comes with a slow learning capability. If the learning capability is too rapid it might not develop an appropriate sort of system, perhaps one that had no stable states.

Anderson

I think there is one other thing that might be said in regard to Eric's comment. It seems that the circuitry of the brain itself is also a learning process: that the brain in the earliest stages, in a few months or years of childhood, is in the process of rewiring itself. Until we can introduce learning machines that can learn to wire themselves, we are probably not going to be able to produce brains.

Freeman

Certainly there is a massive modification of wiring in the nervous system, partly by strengthening pre-existing connections, partly by weakening and wholesale death of nerve cells. This process takes place right from the first laying down of nerve cells in utero, and is of major importance all through childhood. It is important to realize that modification continues on into the later decades of life, so that those of us who sit on this panel and are facing our declining years can have some hope of continued refinement of our connections!

I think the emphasis on connectivity is to a certain extent misplaced, if it is thought of in terms of ourselves re-wiring our machines, or improving on the wiring from outside. The learning process involves modifications, which are internally organized. Further, I would say that there is one feature, for the guidance of wiring, which I see as lacking emphasis; this is the role of action, of movement into the environment by biological systems, and comparably so in computer systems; i.e. robots. After all, plants don't have nervous systems, but animals do, and the main function of these nervous system is to produce action, and the most significant action is to seek input. It is the interplay of action and sensory impact that guides the wiring of neural connections.

Perception really begins as a process of motor command for action within the brain. Some movement of the sensors and positioning of the input channels is ordered at the same time that a command (what biologists call a re-afferent message) goes to all the sensory systems to announce that a change in sensory inflow is about to take place. Sensory cortexes take advantage of this to recognize the effects of the body's own actions, so that if a sound appears, it may or may not be from one's own voice, and so forth. The message, then, is that the nervous system is modifying itself through actions on the environment. And, as a general principle for the development of intelligence machines, that is to say, true artificial intelligence, it seems to me that this closure of the loop of action by the machine into the environment and then back again through its sensors is a crucial problem. Certainly this is being addressed to a certain extent in the design and development of robots which are given actions to do and which have the problem of sorting out the effects on their sensory input of their own actions versus the changes which are taking place in the world outside as it continues to evolve. I think that this is the aspect of the intelligence and even of the Big-C "Consciousness", which arises in brains as a result of this operation of action, re-afference sensory testing, and so forth. That is a dimension of computers which needs to be explicitly addressed.

Carlo Sequin (University of California, Berkeley)

I was intrigued by the fact that Bill Gear brought up the article in the January 1990 issue of Scientific American. In this article, John Searle gives a very easy answer to the question whether computers can "think." Searle essentially defines "thinking" as the process occurring in the biological substance that our brains are made of; anything that is not of that substance cannot "really" think; so, obviously, computers cannot think! It is a very tight circular argument. I was so incensed by it, that I wrote four separate letters to the editors with various levels of sarcasm, but I am not sure whether one of them is mellow enough so that it can actually be printed.

But now I want to keep my comments more concrete and specifically address a question to Walter Freeman. We have seen that there is a lot of overlap in the capabilities of the traditional Von Neuman computer and the capabilities of neural networks. The former can simulate such nets with varying degrees of detail and efficiency. However, this morning, Walter showed us the important role that chaotic processes play in biological systems, and that such processes can also be used in a very beneficial way for some industrial part identification task. This demonstration of the usefulness of chaotic processes introduces an aspect of computing that certainly has not yet been exploited on the kind of computing typically done in Von Neuman machines. Thus, I would like to hear Walter's comments on how much of a new dimension of computing such chaotic processes might add, and whether perhaps they add something that is fundamentally new.

Freeman

Yes, there are some fundamental attributes which the chaotic processes can provide. One is a kind of indeterminacy of the future output. We all talk about trial and error in the formation of a learning scheme, so we try things out, try this, try that, but we don't really address the question: where do these trials come from by which we make errors? Certainly some form of generator of outward probes is necessary as the basis for making trials which have never been tried before. A chaotic generator is necessary for that kind of process. Second, chaos can provide for a degree of stabilization of a system in the control of its movement, and that is by providing a broad spectrum. This can be seen in the analysis of patterns of tremor in people with Parkinson's Disease. In the case of a normal individual you have a broad spectrum tremor which can be conceived as having many frequencies which prevent the locking of the system into any one orbit or local limit cycle. In some sense, there is a degeneration of this control system in Parkinson's Disease, which leads to the emergence and then dominance of one frequency. Then the system becomes locked into an abnormal pattern of high amplitude oscillation, rigidity, and lack of the flexibility which characterize normal adaptive behavior. Third, in the mathematical sense there is the finding, emphasized by Shaw, that chaotic processes not only destroy information but in some sense create information. This comes from the sensitivity to initial conditions, so that the longer a process evolves, the less one knows about the details of its initial condition. That is a metaphor for what chaos offers in the way of the adaptiveness and flexibility of this nervous system for adaptation to unpredictable future conditions. It really consists of creation of new patterns. Certainly we see this directly in these spatial patterns of brain activity which emerge within animals. They are fully deterministic, and there is nothing stochastic or magical about them. They come out of the animals on past experience and are not driven by stimulus input. That is a feature which is, I think, very significant in terms of the design in building of systems which can do this.

I submit that it will not be possible to make systems which operate as brains do, simply on limit cycle and equilibrium attractors, but that it will be possible to do this when chaotic dynamics is explicitly introduced into the machinery.

Sequin

I would like to follow another line of daring – and perhaps crazy – thoughts. Many people grant that machines might be able to "think," as long as "thinking" is limited to a very rational, almost mathematical process. But most of the same people would also say that computers could never be "creative." Earlier we have discussed chaotic processes which, in principle, could be used to make random associations between items in a knowledge-base, and thus could explore various pieces of some vast association space more or less by chance. Such mechanisms seem to give us the possibility of creating an "idea generator" that could function as the "heart" of a machine that exhibits some form of creativity. The idea generator would spew out a stream of random associations. These would be passed through a sequence of ever higher-level and more critical filters. The first ones reject all trivial associations that might just be based on the similarity of the sounds of two words. After a few such filters, only associations would be left over that have some non-trivial, and possibly new, semantic content. These would then be subjected to the highest levels of critical analysis, where they might be checked whether they hold up against the laws of physics and whether they might have some useful application. More than 99% of all associations may be filtered out early as garbage, and less than 1% may ever make it through to reach some higher level of sensibility analysis; but still after millions of cycles one should expect that some concept is generated that is potentially useful.

Any feelings, Walter, on whether such a mechanism might actually work?

Freeman

This is a lovely idea. Then the filter obviously is in the environment feeding back onto the machine. What works is creative; what doesn't work is nonsense.

Amari

The modern computer is a finite state machine, so, in principle, it cannot generate a chaotic behavior. However, we can simulate chaotic dynamics by using modern computers as precisely as possible. Therefore, the problem is how to recognize that we have created something interesting by quasi-chaotic dynamics in a computer or in the brain. So we need another principle to understand what is interesting and creative and what isn't.

Ira Jacobs (Virginia Polytechnic Institute and State University)

Philip Anderson raised the question of the difficulty of machines being able to learn how to wire themselves. Is that really so difficult if you separate the physical wiring from the logical wiring? One can have very simple physical wiring that permits a vast array of possible logical wiring that indeed can be learned.

H. T. Kung (Carnegie-Mellon University)

I think when we talk about wiring and about chaos, we need to know how much creativity we're asking for. There are small creativities and there are large ones. Small creativities are easy. You just need to do a small amount of "learning", that is, get to some local minimum by a simple learning process – you will get there right away. However, if you want to do global learning it is very, very difficult by definition, I think. Therefore we need to specify, when we talk about learning, whether we are addressing difficult learning or easy learning. Can anybody help me on this? Give me a definition of the complexity of the different levels of learning?

Baum

I don't know if there is a sharp dividing line, but leaving that question aside just for a minute, let me answer the prior speaker and Phil Anderson. There is, of course, a necessity for us to build machines which will then wire themselves. That was the first part of my comment that neural networks' main contribution was to focus on learning. In fact chips are not only on the drawing board but actually exist which wire themselves now. They are not very effective at it but it's certainly something which is not only possible, but in existence.

Cary Kornfeld (NEC Research Institute)

One of the things that strikes me here is one of the points that Walter brings up: the system we call the mind is highly distributed and has a very distributed control structure, a cooperative structure. It is influenced by many factors. Some of them are directly wired and some not so directly related, such as the hormone level in which our body determines our mood in some way and provides another dimension that we never achieve in a digital, hardwired computer. I think that this issue of cooperative control is the central and key difference between biological and digital systems.

Freeman

Certainly the question of wiring is a bit of a red herring in the sense of that during embryonic and fetal growth there is a proliferation of nerve cells and an immense number of connections is formed. The process continues after birth with more and more connections. What is modifiable is the strength of these connections. It's modifiable in two places. One, as you say is by a hormonal action at particular synapses in conjunction with reinforcement, that is, with pleasure and pain, and the other is a virtually instantaneous change which can take place by bias current at the trigger zones where conversion is done from waves to pulses. Bias current can immediately change the intensity or the strength of connections, so rewiring can be simulated, I think, most directly by having hybrid types of machines, which have essentially locked-in analog lines, and connection weights that can be changed at will by use of digital memory stores.

Nakata (NEC C&C System Research Laboratories)

I have a question related to a comment of Professor Kung. The recognition of the sounds made by people might be executed at lower level of cognition using pattern matching done with very many brain cells matching local knowledge. On the other hand, there might be enough computational hierarchy above to store the lower patterns which match and create a sequential thought pattern from them because it seems that people think sequentially. So I wonder if there might be two hierarchies, one at a low level doing pattern matching in parallel and one at a higher level operating sequentially?

Kung

I think it's clear that low level stuff is more parallel and high level stuff more sequential. I have been helping the vision people to do some parallel processing. The more I work with them, the more I realize the difficulty of the problem. The problem is not just that we can define levels. It's really the interactions between high level and low levels. Somehow the low level processing gives high level insights. The high level symbolically processes them, and then directs the low level processing to focus on certain areas that need to be examined more carefully. This interaction is really the hardest thing.

Amari

Also I think that symbolic thinking has a large influence on pattern thinking. But this usually is carried out in the subconsciousness, so we cannot explain its processes. What we recognize is just the sequential thinking. When I speak, as I am doing now, I'm speaking in sequential symbols. However, my thinking includes many levels, and most are processed in parallel, so I also believe that both sequential thinking and pattern thinking go together in a mutually interacting way.

Now it is time to turn to our second topic. Professor Valiant will introduce this topic, and Professor Kung will respond.

2 Topic 2: The Future of Parallelism

Introduction   Professor Valiant
Response   Professor Kung

Valiant

I have no doubt that special purpose computers are going to get faster and faster, and that they will use parallelism to achieve this. The question I'd like to ask the panel is whether parallel multiprocessing machines will ever become a norm in general purpose computation, and even possibly replace the von Neuman model, which is the current norm.

First we have to ask whether general purpose parallel computation is possible at all. Certainly, I know of no serious theoretical impediments although people have tried to find them. There is a pragmatic case sometimes put forward favoring only special purpose exploitation of parallelism, and this is based essentially on the high costs of communication. Whether this case has ever had validity is debatable, but currently with the promise of optical communication, its force must be diminishing. Suppose, therefore, that we accept the possibility of general purpose parallel computers. We are then left with the problem of envisaging the process that would make it a reality. What would it take, for example, for systematic use of multiprocessing to become the norm in, say, desktop machines?

The only way I see this coming about is by the general community reaching agreement on some standard model of parallel computing, a model that would provide a standard interface between software and hardware. The advantages of such a standard are clearly that it would make possible the separation of development of software and hardware, much as the von Neuman model does sequential computing. Therefore, I am advocating as a research area the investigation of such models. What is needed, I believe, is some consensus at this conceptual level, before general purpose parallel computers can become a reality and take off and challenge the sequential market.

I think that as long as no consensus emerges, multiprocessor parallelism will remain an exotic side show. Personally, I found it instructive to look back at the early history of sequential computers and ask whether these had arisen out of some such conceptual consensus, rather than from a sequence of engineering improvements. Maurice Wilkes who is credited with having made the first working stored program computer back in 1949, makes some illuminating references to this question in his book, "Memoirs of A Computer Pioneer[3]." He first became a computer academic in Cambridge, England as early as 1937. He recalls how in 1946, a visitor back from the United States put in his hands a document written by von Neuman on behalf of the group at the Moore School entitled, "A Draft Report on the EDVAC". He sat up late into the night to read it since copiers didn't exist at that time. In the report, he said, "clearly laid out were the principles on which development of the modern digital computer was to be based," the stored program, serial execution, binary switching, etc. He writes "I recognized this at once as the real thing and from that time on never had any doubts as to the way computer development would go." There is a second relevant and haunting passage later in his book, also referring to the same year, 1946, where he says "by that time the unique and fruitful interlude when contributions to computer design could be made by both mathematicians and engineers was over. The initiative now lay with the engineers exclusively. Their task was to build a working computer that would embody the ideas that had been jointly evolved." So my question to all of you is whether what we need is not a conceptual advance or consensus of an analogous nature to that arrived at in the 1940's. Will there be a 1946 for parallelism, and when?

Kung

I am not sure whether or not the question you are asking is relevant, namely, if parallel processing machines will be general purpose or not. Parallel processing will be successful without being general purpose, just like our brain, which is, in fact, very special purpose. If we have cases where parallel processing does much better than any other approach that we know of, we will be successful. We don't need to do everything well. So the issue is really performance. The fundamental reason that people use parallel processing is speed. If you want speed, the only way you can do it is to make sure that the problems are regular, that the communication can be handled, and that the locality is preserved, etc. If you can take advantage of all the structure you can get from the computation, you can get the ultimate speed-up.

Communication is not going to be solved by optical methods alone. We know it is not possible because of delays due to the speed of light. Moreover, optics are not going to solve all communication problems because we still need to face resource contention issues. You just cannot use everything in parallel. There are communications that have to be done one after another because of resource contention. It is very nice if you can always bring a copy of data to your local machine. As a result, you can read it independently from other people's use of the copy. So there are certain circumstances in which you just have to be willing to do special things, for example, preserve

---

[3]MIT Press, Cambridge, MA, 1985.

locality. If you start to destroy locality, for example, to randomize location, you are not going to get any speed. This is because you lose all the structure you had in the first place. So I don't feel sorry at all if parallel processing does not handle general processing. Instead of fighting with Crays or fighting with all these wonderful RISC machines, I will cooperate with them. I'm going to send all the problems that cannot be parallelized well to sequential machines. I'll leave the nice regular problems to myself. For these problems by using parallel machines I will do a hundred times, a thousand times, better and eventually I'm going to scale the machines up so that with little effort I can even win by factors of millions.

Comments from panel members and audience

Tarjan

I think it's clear that sequential machines are not going to be replaced by parallel machines. The interesting intellectual question is where is the boundary that defines what parallel machines can do substantially better than sequential machines? What kinds of computations cannot be parallelized and what kinds of computations can be parallelized? I think that there are many kinds of computations, including many of the most computation-intensive tasks that people are trying to do that can be parallelized. Computations in fluid dynamics, in computational chemistry, and in biological sequence analysis are eminently parallelizable. There are many things that are not so easy to parallelize, including important, computationally intensive tasks. I think the jury is still entirely out on whether certain kinds of searching tasks such as arise in AI can be made parallel or not.

There are many interesting challenges in trying to push the boundaries of parallelism: just how much regularity do you need, what kind of regularity do you need, how far can you go in the direction of using parallelism in interesting kinds of computations?

Valiant

I think the situation is not just a competition between one kind of sequential machine and one kind of parallel machine. The problem with parallelism at the moment is that there are a large number of proposals for parallel machines, which are competing against each other. What holds back the advance of parallel computers is that there isn't a clear direction of development. I don't think that the main issue, although certainly a very interesting question, is the boundary between using one processor and more than one processor. I think the big question is whether parallel computers will remain forever rather specialized machines, each appropriate only for special problems and requiring programming by highly skilled programmers.

Tarjan

Do you believe that there is one model of parallelism out there that everyone can agree on, especially if the issue is raw speed?

Valiant

I think that the main issues are raw speed on the one hand and programmability on the other. I also think that it is important to look for a model to agree on because agreeing on a standard, even one which no one likes entirely, has enormous benefits.

Kung

I think the picture is pretty clear. There are not too many parallel machines around currently. On one class of machines, the so-called data-parallel machines, you just have to do the straightforward transformation: you partition the data space into chunks and run them in parallel. The other kind of parallel machines are a little more general, namely you can also partition the computation, as well as the data.

Baum

I think one can make a case that the nuclear power industry in this country was doomed by settling on one model too early: I wouldn't like to see that happen to parallel computing. As to whether AI questions can be parallelized, they are presumably solved by the brain which has a 10 milli-second time scale, so if they can't be parallelized, then we really are in trouble.

Tarjan

I would say it depends upon the computational task. Certainly perception, if you regard that as part of AI, is obviously highly parallel. But consider chess playing, theorem proving, logical deductions, and sequential thinking processes. It is not so obvious of how much of these tasks goes on in parallel in the human brain.

Koseki (NEC C&C Systems Research Laboratories)

I have a naive and simple question for researchers in parallelism. It is: why are you only emphasizing the speed-up of parallelism? I think that if one could realize simpler programming, reliability, or adaptability by utilizing parallelism, one would have a new generation of computing. Maybe one could implement a general purpose machine utilizing these capabilities.

Kung

The answer is easy: speed was the original reason people went to parallelism. That was the only reason in the beginning. After they got speed, they asked for other stuff. If they just want the other stuff, they would never go to parallel processing in the first place, because reliability or simpler programming is much more easily achieved on sequential machines.

Peter Wolff (NEC Research Institute)

What happens if you try to solve a problem which is ill-suited to parallel computing with a parallel computer? What is the manifestation that's going wrong? How does it fail?

Tarjan

One answer is that you'll get slow down instead of speed up!

Ogielski

Following Les Valiant's statement, I want to add an historical anecdote and suggest a look from a different perspective. In the 1940's it was by no means clear to everybody that the establishment of standards for a stored program computer would be a real breakthrough. There was a very strong opposition to von Neuman's ideas, amongst others from Harvard's patron saint, Howard Aiken, whose view at the time was that writing programs would take orders of magnitude more time than actual computing. Ironically, today this happens to be a common argument against parallel machines. This may be due to a lack of standards, as you said, or because it is just difficult, or because a lot of programs are not directly parallelizable. However, to say that something cannot be done on parallel machines is like proving nonexistence theorems, and it's not easy. The boundary between what can and what cannot be done in parallel is constantly moving.

Perhaps we should relax a little and let the time take its course. Very few people expected in the 40's and early 50's that first computers would eventually become general purpose machines. Certainly Aiken did not: at the beginning he saw computers primarily as machines for computing function tables.

Kung

I agree with you. However, the problem you are addressing is a problem you created for yourself. We never claimed that parallel processing is going to do everything. If you want to make parallel processing do things which are inherently not suitable for parallel processing, you'll end up with all these difficulties. The important thing is to find problems which are inherently parallelizable. For those problems, the programming will be much, much easier than you thought. Make sure that we do those problems first. There are enough of them to keep us busy.

Mitchell Marcus

I have a question. For lots of real problems, it's not hard after just a little thought to see what a data parallel solution would look like, allowing a simple solution on some hypothetical MIMD machine. I don't understand, for real world problems, what makes it hard to decide, at least naively, about whether something is parallelizable or not. In other words, let's say that one just had several machines of different architectures to use, and had a small problem that one wanted to program up in, say, an afternoon. If we had been brought up in several different paradigms, rather than just understanding simple serial machines, would it be clear to us what to do for most real problems or would it be difficult? Is there something fundamentally hard about the deciding about whether something parallelizable or not? I don't understand where the difficulty is.

Joan Feigenbaum (AT&T Bell Laboratories, Murray Hill)

This is a naive answer: Whether or not it is hard depends on what you mean by parallel machines, but, say, for the PRAM model of parallel machines, there is a very precisely stateable unsolved theoretical problem of whether or not P = NC, and many, many real problems are hard to prove to be members of NC or to be P-complete. So, I think that it's not at all obvious which problems are parallelizable and which ones aren't in that model. If you take another model, whatever model it is, why should it be obvious which problems are parallelizable in that model?

Lee Giles (NEC Research Institute)

I'd like to bring up another model of parallelism which actually works continuously in the environment. It's called the social insects. They are parallel autonomous systems that are very adaptive. They perform many very interesting tasks, all in real time, adapting to changing environs. Do you think that as a model, we have anything useful to learn about parallel computing from them? A related area would be the work of Bernard Huberman[4] on collective computation. As an example, Huberman discusses traffic lights coordinating themselves, talking to themselves and managing traffic flow. A very serious problem, as we all know, but that should be manageable.

---

[4] B. A. Huberman and T. Hogg, "The behavior of computational ecologies," in *The Ecology of Computation*, ed. B. A. Huberman, North Holland, 1988.

Ogielski

About social insects: yes, there is a similar computer model[5]. In a beautiful body of recent work on bees it has been shown that, apart from already known chemical signs and dancing, the bees also communicate indirectly as follows: They can perceive a job that has not been finished (such as nest construction etc.) or that needs more bees for completion, and this is the cue to pick up work and continue. This is like a kind of bulletin-board model of distributed programming, in which there is a list of jobs to be done, and processors check it from time to time and perhaps pick up the next job. This is one of the standard models, and it should have the collective behavior and adaptive character associated with at least some aspects of insect life, to the extent that we know it.

Nakata

I've been working on parallel processing systems for 5 years or so, and, from my experience, what is parallelizable and what is not mainly depends on the data dependencies. If there are enough independencies that the task can be divided into processes, then they can be parallelized. Currently, the difficult job is the determination of the data dependencies, either by a very clever compiler or by the programmer. So, I think that the question asked by Professor Valiant might be answered by specifying how one defines the data dependency of a program, and also how one goes about determining that data dependency.

Valiant

Clearly there are some difficult intellectual questions regarding what can and cannot be computed efficiently in parallel. Still I think what holds back parallel computing isn't this problem. Among the large numbers of computations people would like to perform efficiently, many can be parallelized very easily. Yet there is neither a large software industry producing software for parallel machines nor are many parallel machines sold and used. I think the reason for this is simply that no one is going to put effort into writing large programs if they don't have some confidence that people are going to use them. If they have to write them for one particular machine which may disappear in 6 months time, they will not do so. Similarly people will not buy machines in large numbers if the software isn't there to run on them.

In the sequential world it is the symbiosis between software and hardware that makes possible the production of both in the large quantities in which they are produced. I've been to parallel conferences for a number of years, and we do not seem to have progressed far towards a large transportable

---

[5]T. D. Seely, "The honey bee colony as a superorganism," *Am. Scientist* **77** (1989) pp 546-553.

software base or towards general purpose parallel machines.

Kung

You have to be really careful how you say things: don't use engineering reasons to beat people up! Consider the microprocessor technology in the early 70s. Microprocessors then were programmed only in assembly code and were used mainly in process control. Any computer scientist seriously using microprocessors was considered very weird. New technologies take some time to mature. Consider another case – vector super computers. When the CDC Star and the TIASC came out in the early 70s, they were extremely difficult to use. When CRAY I came out in 1976, it was still difficult to use. Absolutely no software. It took the Livermore/Los Alamos people 10 years to fix it, but now look: those super computers are real. They solve real problems. You have to give new machines and ideas the time. It took 15 years for vector machines to really make it. Why do we believe parallel processing will mature in less time? I will be happy if we make it after 30 years.

Michael Merritt (Member Technical Staff, AT&T Bell Laboratories)

I'd like to challenge you with a more pessimistic view of the future. Instead of an integrated, fully distributed network of the kind that Professor Kung described yesterday, what we will see is much more likely to be something like a higher performance version of what people have today. Most work is done on resources held locally, in part because of performance, economic, and organizational reasons, but also because of technical problems. These technical problems are not just those of creating software to connect these machines, but problems related to maintaining these systems and the importance of having control over those resources one needs.

There will be some use of very high performance parallel machines, essentially via rlogin sessions over the network, but by no means as a transparent interaction with an abstraction. Instead, we will engage in very conscious interactions with a particular notion of a vector processor or other kind of architecture. Rather than striving towards a single standard in parallel computing, we should be looking towards a small family of such standards that would be accessed in this mode. If we could focus on such a short-term goal, then we might see more progress and the kind of leverage you get with large groups of people working toward developing software for specific architectures. This would give us the kind of explosion in parallel computing that we've seen in sequential computing.

Freeman

Particularly in terms of building many small families, it seems to me that we do in fact need a proliferation of many areas of different types of computing, especially at this stage of early evolution. You might see us as being in the challenge of an ice age, where we get isolated into small groups. This is an optimum strategy for the rapid evolution of new systems: when the ice retreats (meaning when the funds begin to flow again) we can go back into direct competition and see the fittest system survive. But in the meantime there is a great virtue, so to speak, in working at our benches and keeping our minds on the individual and even idiosyncratic avenues that we are trying to explore.

I see as an outsider that this question of serial versus parallel has been drawn too narrowly. Lee Gile's comment about the possibility of using other models such as social insects or traffic management raises the issue into a larger area. Essentially parallel systems can be viewed as, let's say, glorified pipe lines, and that is a very narrow kind of a view. What the idea of social insects raises is that such systems are semi-autonomous and organize themselves through cooperation. These systems need not be parallel, but if self-organization is the key component for the future development of new systems, then they must be in parallel.

I would like also to take this opportunity to comment on something that Professor Valiant brought up about the history of these machines. By 1946 von Neuman had pretty well laid out the program that was then to be followed and he did this explicitly in terms of neural metaphors. He was very strongly influenced by the concepts that dominated our picture at that time, 40 years ago, how brains work. They were wrong, that is to say the ideas were incomplete, ill-formulated, and overly abstract, but very powerful nonetheless.

At the same time, those concepts gave rise to ideas which now appear as neural networks, so both the serial and parallel architectures in computation are the product of misconceptions in neurobiology some 40 years ago. Now we have in fact some advances in our field; we're not as ignorant as we were then, although we still don't have anything like complete knowledge. Much of what we now know in fact has been the fruit of development of computers, which have allowed us to see the forest for the trees. It seems to me that rather that couching this dichotomy strictly in terms of serial versus parallel, it should be done in terms of forward command architectures versus feedback semi-autonomous systems which have their own logic and their own patterns of evolution.

Valiant

I certainly agree that the aim is to get the right models in the end and there may be many ways of getting there. The choices that we do have are in the models we study as researchers. One line of research in parallel computing is to pursue models which we know are special purpose, where the structure of the problem computed is reflected in the connection pattern of the machine. That's a definite choice in research approach. Here I'm advocating a different avenue, aimed at models that are designed to be general purpose.

Gear

Let me address the issue of the software base brought up by Valiant. The fact is that massively parallel computers are not really used for many problems yet. I think it is useful to look back to the period of the early 50's when the serial computer was first coming into use. There was no software base then, there were very few computers around, and computers were relatively little used at first. To some extent these are the same statement: as the software base grew people started to produce copies of the existing machines, and as more machines existed, the software base grew, all in response to the need to solve problems unsolvable by other techniques. The question was, did the importance of the problem justify the effort of generating software. I think that will be the key issue for parallel computers.

As Kung pointed out, problems have been important enough that people have generated the software for super computers. I don't know whether the same will be true in massively parallel computers or not. I think it will depend on whether massively parallel computing appears to be capable of continued evolution to provide the opportunity to solve problems more rapidly than on other types of computers. If that appears to be the case, it will be worth investing the effort to develop the software base. If not, we will not see a software base develop.

Kung

I believe that the collection of problems where parallel processing is ideally suited is very big. So big that the software base will be developed, and that over time people like Professor Valiant and other people will be able to devise more general models. As a result the usage will be enlarged. In the beginning we are going to work on computations we really know how to parallelize. I think that this set of computations is already big enough. After you have solved differential equations with two dimensions, you want to do the same thing in three and four dimensions, and so on. Doing this extension is trivial, really. Many problems with parallel machines today are not because parallelism is hard, they are because these new machines are expensive and flaky. It takes some time to get them to be cost effective and to be reliable enough.

Amari

I have one point. We think in a sequential manner, but an animal does not process information in a sequential manner by using symbols. Originally the brain developed to process information in a parallel manner, but it took many years of evolution for the human being to think in a sequential manner. On the other hand, we have developed a machine which does information processing in an sequential manner. Now we are thinking about the opposite direction: to construct a machine which works in parallel. It took a long time for the parallel machine of the brain to invent a serial mechanism in the development of the brain. Maybe some serious difficulty also exists in the reverse direction of implementing parallel mechanisms in the dominating serial paradigm. If we want to parallelize a serial task, keeping its information structure, it might be very difficult. So in order to parallelize, we need to adopt a very different information representation. In a sequential machine, information is always represented by symbols, a very concentrated information representation. However, if we use a very diffuse, distributed information representation, maybe we'll come up with some different aspect of parallel information processing.

Merritt

I want to follow up on a point that is being brushed under the rug here. That is, apart from the problem of writing software for parallel architectures, or avoiding the problem of writing software by having machines that self organize or program themselves, there is the problem that this software or these machines have to be managed. It is not the case that the program has been written and that's the end of it. We will be faced with the problems of debugging, maintaining, and managing systems that are running such incredibly complicated programs. In my laboratory, we already have highly trained professionals who are there just to make a comparatively simple network of sequential machines run very well-understood sequential programs. They are constantly running around making the whole system work, and I think that it is very naive to think that these problems will not become incredibly more difficult if the machines themselves are highly parallelized. If the machines are self organized so we don't have the foggiest idea of how they are producing whatever output they are producing, that will not make these everyday problems go away, it's going to aggravate them. That is part of the reason why this kind of architecture is going to remain special purpose, because the practical overhead of making it work to solve your problems will be enormous. If we don't focus more attention on these very practical issues, then we will not break through into making a difference for people who have real problems to solve.

Kung

Well I agree with you, but I sense that you are negative, and that's the part that I don't accept. You have to recognize that our ability in dealing with software has increased tremendously over the years. It's true we now deal with programs we never thought we could have dealt with ten, fifteen years ago. We deal with networks, which are self organizing, literally. We have nodes connecting to the network even without network users knowing it. We achieve this by providing more redundancy and checking. It's just that we are sensitive to these software issues but they are not going to kill the whole thing.

S. Goto (NEC C&C Information Technology Research Laboratories)

I like parallel machines, but I believe every problem, once it's formulated in a mathematical way can be solved by sequential machines or sequential algorithms. The merit of parallel machines is the reduction of computation time. Is there any problem, formulated in a mathematical way, which a sequential machine cannot solve, but a parallel machine can?

Kung

Such a problem cannot exist. A sequential machine can always simulate a parallel computation.

Sequin

The question of whether a particular problem can be solved by simulation on a serial computer is not the only issue. I am thinking of a very special purpose machine, the GF11, which is built explicitly to help the physicists understand the structure of the proton from first principles in quantum electro dynamics. If one tried to solve that problem on the fastest sequential machines today, it would take us several decades. The physicists working on this would very much like to get the answer while they are still alive! So they don't mind investing a year or two to build such a special machine.

Anderson

Another answer is: Has anyone really formulated the perception problem that the human eye goes through in mathematical terms, and if so can the problem be solved sequentially? I don't believe that perception is basically possible at all sequentially. One must refer back to the object itself and respond mechanically. Many of the perceptual jobs the body actually does very easily. In fact, worms do them; very low animals with very little circuitry.

Freeman

I want to reinforce the notion that, when we are dealing with arrays of receptors numbering on the order of 10^8, it is absurd to think of doing serial scanning to convert such input to a one-dimensional data string. In the sensors of insects, vertebrates and the U.S. Navy, parallelism is here to stay. I would like to respond to Mike Merritt's comments raising the issue of maintenance. Certainly this is a major problem in biological systems, in fact, we spend roughly a third of our time and perhaps more than half in the routine maintenance of our brains by sleep and other forms of rest and recreation. This is a nontrivial problem, but I would submit that there is a remarkable tolerance to faults in parallel systems. This might be seen best at the manufacturing level, when you have a large number of elements that are subject to error in the manufacturing process. If the system now is to be self organized according to certain simple algorithms which are carried out in an iterative manner, then the system can conceivably be designed to organize itself around these imperfections, and therefore increase the yield of chips.

I think that kind of thinking can be extended onto the maintenance of a system. Obviously our brains are subject to all kinds of insults and trauma which we manage to recover from. If the core algorithms are built in as part of the self-organization, then that should not make the problem by any means go away, but make it manageable.

Merritt

To respond to that response, I suggest that it's very likely the software-engineering problem will be solved by utilizing tools of psychology. I wonder if, in the drive towards replicating biological systems, we aren't just asking to inherit all of the faults of such systems as well as their strengths.

Freeman

Let me say, I am in no sense advocating replication of biological systems. We have far more fun replicating them in other ways. I do think that we can usefully learn some of the fundamental principles. It's not a question of building an airplane that flaps its wings, but rather understanding what some of these elementary principles are. I submit that one of the best ways is do it like Orville and Wilber Wright did, go and watch birds.

Merritt

But I wonder if some of these strengths come with inherent weaknesses. The evolutionary process developed the human brain over a great period of time – if it were an easy task to filter out some of the drawbacks, wouldn't that have happened? Perhaps it is a necessary aspect of human information processing that we spend half of our time asleep. Might not it cut back on the efficiency of electronic information processing systems if they spend all their time asleep?

Freeman

Certainly, I find that there are only three or four hours a week when our Berkeley Computer Center is down for preventive maintenance. I think that Carlo Sequin commented also on the odious nature of what might be called biological chauvinism, to suppose that hydrocarbons are a better basis or the only kind of system that can be made to think. There are in fact, many Achilles heels or deficits in the biological system which might better be handled in other techniques. The greater part of neurobiology is dealing with janitorial aspects of maintenance of the brain. After all, it has to keep itself in good shape for 70, 80, 90 years. Much of its biochemical machinery is devoted to maintaining stability, keeping out bugs, and so forth. We have to do this for our machines now. Those janitorial aspects of neurobiology are irrelevant to the concerns of making new machines and should not be allowed to intrude. The comment was made earlier today that neurons are immensely complex. Yes, they are. The more you look at them, the more the complexity deepens, but those aspects which are relevant to information management and processing are in fact much simpler. There are good reasons for that which have to do with the way neurons smooth and filter as they integrate.

Sequin

You mentioned that humans need to sleep about one third of the time in order to do some internal physiological and psychological maintenance. So one third of our "systems time" can be considered "overhead." Well, there is a nice analogy: There are some fault-tolerant systems that rely on triple modular redundancy. In these systems the output from some sub-system is a majority vote on the outputs of three identical sub-systems that operate in parallel. As long as at least two of each of these redundant sub-systems produce the same outputs, the computation can go on. So here is an example of a system where at least two thirds of all system cycles are overhead in order to achieve reliability. For certain applications we are quite willing to pay this overhead.

Amari

Professor Goodman had to leave earlier, but he had one question to ask Professor Kung which I will read: "Could you enumerate, in order of importance, the current limits to achieving arbitrarily high levels of parallelism in computing systems?"

Kung

I think the real limit is probably the speed of light. Basically current computers are bound by the speed of light already. If you want a machine which has more and more processors, by definition the size gets bigger and bigger. That's the reason why CRAY does not get smaller and smaller over the time. I think that's really the problem, that's the number one. The second is packaging. Basically, you want to reduce the capacitance.

Ogielski

I want to add to what you said. My colleagues in physics who build special purpose computers have found that their lifetime would not be long enough to solve quantum chromodynamics with a GF11 or similar machine. The plan conceived at Columbia and elsewhere is to build a teraflop machine using today's technology, somewhat in the spirit of large scale projects in elementary particle physics.

There are a lot of serious problems with that, such as the need to own a power plant, etc., but what we should stress here is component failure. It is easy to estimate probabilities: A machine with tens of thousands of very complex VLSI processors would fail very often. They need error-correcting processors and error-correcting machines.

The general ideas are already in place (and can be traced back to von Neuman, again), but error-correcting processors cannot easily be bought. A question to H. T. Kung: What do you do about this? Scaling up to 64 chips, that's not a problem yet, but there are guys who dream about really big machines.

Kung

Actually, I had a long conversation with Norm Chris of the Columbia project on this particular issue about a month ago. We can basically build this kind of large scale parallel machine today, but the problem is how to make them fault tolerant. We don't have much experience on this subject yet, I agree with you on that. We need to do some experiments. Actually, there are two extreme solutions, both of which appear reasonable. One is to provide redundancy at a very low level such as the chip level, so every chip will be replicated. The other is to provide redundancy at a very high level, say the processor level. When a whole processor fails, you can kick in a spare processor. Both approaches look very reasonable but I can't tell which one is better. I believe currently the latter is better but we don't have much experience. There is a lot of research that needs to be done. I can't give you a straight answer.

Amari

I would like to thank the panelists and the audience very much for their cooperation, I think we have had a very good time and interesting mental exercises. We have had some heated discussions. We have identified many important problems; some of them were answered, but most remain to be answered. As for the future of parallelism, certain problems may be answered in a practical manner in the near future. In the comparison of the brain and computer, there are some difficult questions. Do machines think, and if so, in what sense? Does chaos produce creativity? These questions may remain unanswered even after ten years because the questions depend on the meaning or definition of "think" and "creativity." On the other hand, mutual interactions between symbolism and pattern representation might be answered in the near future in some practical way, I believe.

I believe we are now in a very exciting period and can look forward to great progress on these problems.